BINDING THE DEVIL

Roger Baker was born near Mansfield, Nottinghamshire. He won a scholarship to Nottingham University and after graduating, joined the staff of the *Nottingham Evening Post* as diary editor, theatre critic and music critic. He subsequently joined *The Tatler,* and then *London Life* as features editor. Since 1967 he has worked as a freelance journalist and writer, and contributes regularly to many newspapers, journals and magazines. He is the author of *Drag* and *Dolls and Doll's Houses* and the editor of *The Book of London.*

The cover illustration is taken from a fresco by Mezzasti of St Anthony of Padua, in the Museo of St Anthony, Montefalco, Italy. It is used by permission of the Mansell Collection, London.

BINDING THE DEVIL

Exorcism Past and Present

ROGER BAKER

SHELDON PRESS
LONDON

First published in Great Britain in 1974 by
Sheldon Press, Marylebone Road, London NW1 4DU

Copyright © 1974 Roger Baker

Printed in Great Britain by
Hollen Street Press Limited, Slough

ISBN 0 85969 042 3

CONTENTS

PREFACE

A fundamental belief in the world of spirits can never be entirely eradicated from man's consciousness. In our materialistic and technological world where an explanation can be offered for almost everything, one might expect to find the idea of hauntings, spirits and exorcism laughingly dismissed as so much medieval superstition.

But this is not so. Proof lies in the tremendous growth of interest in the occult which began about ten years ago and reached a significant peak in the early years of the present decade. Exorcism is but one aspect of this interest which embraces the raising of spirits through ouija boards and seances, the participation in black magic and other esoteric cults and foretelling the future by various systems.

That the spirit world retains its power receives support from worldly and practical sources. In Britain a schoolboy charged with setting fire to his school and home was defended on the grounds that he had become possessed — a plea accepted by the court when they heard that the fire-raising had ceased after the boy had been exorcized.

This book is an attempt to explain something of the history and nature of possession and exorcism. An anthropological approach to the subject tends not to allow the existence of demons; a theological approach tends to believe that there is something in it. Here I have tried to present both attitudes fairly. And in the later chapters an answer to the essential question: Does exorcism work? is formulated.

It would be invidious to present a long list of people — priests, psychiatrists, social workers, exorcists and the exorcized — who have been helpful. Sometimes a stray word in conversation is more powerful than a two-hour lecture. But my grateful thanks are extended to all these friendly and sensitive people.

ROGER BAKER

INTRODUCTION

Exorcism is the act of expelling evil spirits from, or out of a person or place by invocation or the use of a holy name. As such, the concept implies far-ranging theories about the nature of evil, and the existence of evil spirits as tangible or personified things. Assumptions must be made, too, about whether such spirits do exist, externally from man, and if so how they might enter a person or place, what they then do, and where they go when expelled.

Exorcism poses other questions related to medicine, psychology and the occult in general. Why are certain individuals infested, as it were, by the wayward spirits and others not? and — at the root of the concept — is it possible to believe that a spiritual being can be transferred from one place to another by ritual?

Rites and forms of worship that have a close assonance with exorcism can be found in all cultures and throughout all ages, but the ritual has always held a particularly special place in Christianity. Christ himself was a powerful and successful exorcist, and the gospels feature prominently, examples of his ability to expel spirits. Taken singly, Christ's exorcisms can be read as occasional magic gestures designed to support his charisma, or they may be interpreted as allegories of good and evil at war in social terms. But an overall view of the New Testament makes two things clear. One is that the exorcisms were real in the documentary sense; and the other is that Christ himself — and his early followers — regarded exorcism, not merely as a piece of dramatic decoration for his teachings, but as an integral part of the on-going

fight against evil that besieges mankind. Christ's function
has been described as that of 'exorcizing a whole culture', and this may also be seen to apply to the function
of Christianity itself: 'And we know we are of God,
and the whole world lies in wickedness'. (1 John 5.19).

This text (and there are many others of similar import) explains why, in the structure of the early Church,
exorcism automatically preceded baptism for the first
neophytes. The assumption was, that since such converts
had, naturally enough, previously adhered to some other
form of religion, usually pagan, they were clearly vulnerable to demons and spirits which they must formally
renounce. But alongside this formal procedure, troubled
individuals — such as those we meet in the gospels —
seem to have been regarded as possessed by devils, and
treated as such.

We learn that official exorcists were appointed, and
part of the Church set aside for their care. Fr J. H. Crehan
S.J. has pointed out that the role of such exorcists was
probably somewhat similar to that of the male nurse.[1]
The possessed were regarded as being part of the Christian
community — that is, not isolated as sick or untouchable
— since this would assist their rehabilitation.

This is, of course, remarkably similar to certain
methods used today by radical therapists who, instead
of handling their patients as individuals needing a
personal therapy for a private neurosis, prefer to see
them as part of the community. And this makes ex-
cellent sense in the Rome of 251 A.D. as much as in our
contemporary world.

As the basic baptism-exorcism ritual — essentially a
purification rite — slipped quietly into common Church
liturgies the ideas surrounding Satan himself grew in
stature particularly through the middle ages and the
concept of satanic possession demanding individual

exorcism grew, reaching its peak during the witch craze of the sixteenth and seventeenth centuries. The exorcism rituals varied, but were often determined, crude and sometimes cruel, especially in the area of personal assaults on the possessed such as the forcible insertion of enemas, the devil being frequently associated with the bowels.

Exorcisms were frequent during the sixteenth and seventeenth centuries and seemingly haphazard, because anyone could, even accidentally, be accused, tried and possibly exorcized. Pope Urban VIII, however, urged potential exorcists to be guarded in their approach, and to be slow to accept demonic possession. He also evolved some diagnostic guide-lines to determine authentic possession. This attitude is predominant in the Church today. Exorcism is a ritual of last resort and the exorcist is instructed carefully to make sure that all other possible explanations of the patient's behaviour have been explored and rejected.

The *New Catholic Encyclopedia* states: 'Psychiatry has shown that the workings of the subconscious explain many, if not most, of the abnormal activities that earlier generations had attributed to diabolical activity'. And indeed, as our knowledge of psychiatry, parapsychology, telepathy, telekinesis and extra-sensory perception increases, so the diagnosis of possession must become even more astringent. What is known as 'speaking in tongues' — that is, a sudden fluency in a language that the subject could never have learned in the normal way — and the acquisition of enormous strength were both regarded as essential signs of possession. Yet modern research indicates that both are, under certain conditions, quite scientifically possible and comprehensible.

So as scientific knowledge increases, the possibilities

of extraordinary phenomena being attributed to demonic possession shrink accordingly, until we are left with a small list of manifestations which are, as yet, inexplicable though they may in time receive logical explanation. For these reasons exorcism as a natural part of the repertory of the Church tended to recede in importance until it became almost forgotten. And, as the devil himself began to lose the stature he once had, other reasons were sought for the source of man's inhumanity to man, helped along by the social analysis of Marx and the explorations of the mind conducted by Freud and Jung.

Writing in 1971, the Anglican Bishop of Exeter said: 'The general attitude of the Church of England seemed to be to regard exorcism as an exercise in white magic . . .'.[2] This putting away of exorcism was, perhaps, the inevitable concomitant of a tendency − which some have noted with concern − for the Anglican Church to concentrate its pastoral or grass-roots activities more and more onto a practical level, in social work or community politics, at the expense of attending effectively to man's higher, spiritual needs.

This is, of course, an arguable point but certainly the strenuous efforts made by the Church, in the face of an ever-increasing apostasy, to keep up with the times, has meant a gradual playing down of the mysterious or supernatural elements. Possession tests credulity in this materialistic and technological age; exorcism would, therefore, be among the first of the more spiritual rituals to be set aside. However, in the world at large, the apparent increase of interest in magic, the occult and psychic manifestations, has prompted the Church to look again at this aspect of its work. It was, no doubt, disturbing to see congregations turning to fringe magic or to eastern mystics for the sort of spiritual guidance that the Church itself is well able, by tradition and practice, to supply.

During this century, all the main Christian Churches have taken a similar line on anything that now smacks of the supernatural. When one of the basic theology texts used at the Jesuits' Gregorian University in Rome was revised, the entire section on angels and demons was omitted from the new edition.

But if the Churches decided that demons and angels were no longer relevant, their views were not universally shared and they were, consequently, unprepared for the challenge presented to them by the rise once more of Satanism, forms of witchcraft and a significant leaning towards the occult during the last decade. This is an ironic situation. Reaction to technology and materialism turns the individual towards the search for an other-worldly, spiritual experience as comfort, guide, or even resource. Yet the Churches seem to be neglecting this aspect of their function and so the individual must seek elsewhere. He may turn to hallucinogenic drugs, to dabbling in the occult or to Satanism. Often these experiments are harmless. Sometimes they can reach terrible lengths in ritual murders, as exemplified in the operations of Charles Manson and his 'family'. Sometimes they seem more pathetic in the creation of witch-circles and the unpleasant but probably harmless rituals of necromancy. Sales of packs of Tarot cards escalate and a distinguished Jungian analyst told me that neither she, nor several of her colleagues would start a new day before consulting the I Ching — the Chinese oracle of changes.

At the time of writing, what could be called a witch-craft trial is being held in London. A young man said to be a high priest of the British Occult Society is charged among other things with desecrating graves. It is said that he stole corpses and held nude rituals in a cemetery. According to *The Times* report he claimed that the naked dancing on tombs was 'for exorcism. . .'[3]

Any occult system, or indeed religious system, that espouses the theory of dualism and perceives good and evil as opposing forces (rather than reflections of the same thing, or as in the Old Testament of evil being used by God to test his people) will include rituals of exorcism devised according to their own theories and demonologies. Being altogether outside Christianity their relevance is less important.

Although the rise of interest in the occult and witchcraft has obtruded onto the public consciousness only fairly recently, it did begin to make an impact as long ago as 1963, and, in England, prompted the Church of England to take a fresh look at exorcism.

A Commission was convened by the Bishop of Exeter who wrote: 'I was much disturbed by the unhealthy and near-hysterical publicity given by the national press to the question of exorcism in the Church of England. I was also disturbed by the number of requests for help and advice about the exorcizing of places or persons which I was receiving.'

A similar 'unhealthy and near-hysterical outburst' recurred early in 1974 with the showing of the film *The Exorcist*. The great thunder of old-style Hollywood promotion tactics were revived as first American and then British newspapers sensationalized the film, reporting that it was making more money than any had done previously and that audiences were reacting violently by fainting, screaming, being sick. Almost overnight the word *exorcist* became synonymous with all that was horrific and fearful. The views of priests of all denominations, and those of various experts in the occult, were solicited by magazines and the other media. Those who did not, like Billy Graham, condemn the entire operation as 'spiritual pornography' tended to take it seriously whether they decided that it was an awful warning against dabbling in the occult, or whether they felt it was an admirable demonstration of the power of good over evil.

The film *The Exorcist* is basically no more than a horror movie in the best traditions of Dracula and the 'invasion from outer space' genre of the 1950s. A pretty twelve-year-old girl living in middle-class security begins to develop alarming symptoms after playing with an ouija board. Her distraught mother takes her to a series of brain specialists, psychiatrists and other doctors none of whom can find any physical defect that may explain her behaviour. Eventually an exorcist is recommended and visited. The horror of the film lies in its most certainly expert special effects and make-up departments as the child changes from sweet innocence to a vilely maimed and distorted creature, screaming obscenities, vomiting, speaking with the bass voice of the devil and making her head turn rapidly through 360 degrees.

The exorcism ritual, which is the climax of the film, takes place with repeated prayers and the devil in the child becoming increasingly violent. The exorcist himself dies suddenly of a heart attack, whereupon the young Jesuit priest who has been assisting demands that the devil take *him* over. This apparently happens and the priest then kills himself by leaping from the bedroom window, but is able to receive absolution before he dies.

Clearly, if an event, such as demonic possession, is to be dramatized for a vast popular audience, certain acceptable, fictional structures have to be created. Consequently, the main characters in the film are all rather attractive — the mother, her secretary, the Jesuit priest —

and there is an undertow of sexual tension between them. The idea of the young hero sacrificing himself to save the world from an overwhelming threat is common-place in the science-fiction genre. It was for example, used pertinently, in a British film called *Quatermass and the Pit*, interesting in this context, because that piece, quite powerfully, explored the source of images of the devil and of a certain kind of possession.

However, *The Exorcist* fails to be relevant to exorcism on other grounds. The symptoms acquired by the child are treated almost as though they had a physical cause, and she is kept firmly in her room, later strapped to the bed. Thus we are enticed into the 'monster in the attic' theme and for this reason the film tells us nothing about evil in the theological sense, and the climax emerges as the triumph of ritual over superstition rather than of good over evil. The death of the young priest is strongly reminiscent of the gospel story of the Gadarene swine and is equally mysterious. An important element of Christian exorcism is omitted from the drama: that the possessed person should not only be relieved of the in-festing demon, but that the space left by its expulsion should be filled by the Holy Ghost. The child in *The Exorcist* is virtually ignored in the final struggle, only to be discovered whimpering in a corner with no memory or awareness of what has happened to her.

The symptoms displayed by the girl tell us less about possession than about the cultural assumptions of middle-class America. That the audience gets its collective heart wrung by the prospect of seeing all this violence and brutality inflicted on a sweet little girl is in itself mani-pulative. Some of the actions she performs — such as urinating on the carpet during a smart party, screaming endless obscenities, grabbing a psychiatrist by the testicles and abusing the priest's dead mother are horrible simply because this child is doing them. Were the possessed person a middle-aged man of vagrant background, an alcoholic woman or indeed any figure from outside accepted social norms, then our responses would be radically different.

The film was adapted by William Peter Blatty from his own novel of the same title. And the novel is a slightly different piece of work. Here, the fictional dramatics are accepted (two mild sub-plots surrounding the operations of the local detective) but Blatty goes much further into the causes, the symptoms and the possibilities of demonic possession. The novel is thoroughly researched, informative and although the Gadarene climax remains puzzling it is much more relevant to the mystery of exorcism.

Blatty, it is reported, based his book on an actual case of demonic possession. In 1949 a fourteen-year-old boy from Mount Rainier began to display signs of what is called 'poltergeist phenomena' — that is, furniture and objects around him would move, apparently of their own volition. He yelled curses in dead languages and at one point long red scratches appeared on his body while he was firmly strapped to his bed. Exorcism was finally tried and the Jesuit assigned to the case prepared himself by fasting and eventually worked on the boy for two months, with ceremonies taken from the *Rituale Romanum*. Eventually the climax occured and the possessing spirit identified itself as one of the fallen angels mentioned in the Bible, and departed. All this information has been pieced together from newspaper accounts and unofficial accounts, which may have been sensationalized in places.

A copy of the diary that the priest kept fell into Blatty's hands and from it he created his dynamic novel. Blatty elaborated the course of the possession, adding such details as the swivelling head and the scene in which the girl masturbates crudely with a crucifix. The first was drawn from other documented cases of possession; the latter was his own imaginative detail. Again, in the transference of a male original to a fictional female, one senses a note of opportunism. Many of the demonic symptoms, though no less dreadful, would certainly receive a higher threshold of tolerance were they demonstrated by a young male. And in this context the masturbation scene has a significance. Obviously, such an action could not be attributed to a male in quite the same way, and as in invention it seems a product of a society that has a male-dominated, repressive attitude to female sexuality.

These considerations undermine the viability of the film as a whole, and if there are any arguments about whether the movie is serious or sensational, will provide evidence for the latter verdict. Though so clearly patterned on the familiar horror film, *The Exorcist* lacks the gothic flamboyance of the Dracula variants and replaces it with something peculiarly nasty; whether this nastiness is evidence of the revelation of genuine evil or a simple dip into a certain kind of religious pornography remains highly debatable. But while the film and to a lesser extent the book may be criticized on both theologically and on grounds of commercial exploitation, the concept of exorcism nevertheless caught the public's imagination particularly in America. In fact a curious kind of transference seemed to take place whereby the exorcist himself became the figure of terror rather than the possessed. In a similar way, the name Frankenstein is often used to describe the monster, rather than the well-meaning doctor.

Certainly the hysteria which the film caused in America appears to have been short-lived but it has nevertheless left in its wake a trail of new thoughts: thoughts about the devil, about good and evil, about the possibility of demonic possession. Those who predicted a sharp increase in cases of possession as a result of the film were proved over-enthusiastic. One American newspaper took the whole thing to ludicrous depths by announcing in a dogmatic headline: 'Satan has 80 Horrifying Demons that can Take Possession of Your Body'. Few readers — even in middle America where susceptibility seems particularly strong — would take this information seriously. But the basic idea of exorcism and possession has been quite firmly established and remains to be debated and explored.

When Aldous Huxley published his book *The Devils of Loudon* in 1952 he fixed an image that seemed quite relevant to the age. The longevity of the story and the fact that it continually stimulates artists in different media — drama, the cinema, opera — proves its potency. The theme which caught the imagination was partly that of possession, but more importantly the nature of religious and political persecution. Blatty's work has shifted this emphasis more firmly onto possession and has helped to raise the devil. Why the time was right has yet to be discovered. It has been suggested that people have been encouraged to look once more for the evil that lies inside themselves, and that instead of accepting personal responsibility for it, they have been given the option of putting responsibility firmly onto outside supernatural forces.

In the novel, the possessed girl's mother is portrayed as a nonbeliever in God. 'But the devil keeps advertising . . . the devil does lots of commercials', she says at one point. Perhaps people feeling that the world is in such a terrifying mess and needing to deflect the responsibility from themselves are once more raising the devil to take that responsibility. Professional clerics in

America who welcomed the film hoped that the message would be taken further, and that the answer would be seen as lying not in a quasi-magical ritual but in a return to the Church and to the real power of faith.

Whether this happens remains to be seen. But in a world where superstition seems almost the norm and where faith and reason seem to be in retreat, almost anything is possible. As we shall see, exorcisms today bear little resemblance to the operatic climax of *The Exorcist,* and manifestations of possession while sometimes mysterious and frightening, do not reach the dramatic level of those performed by the film's child-heroine. Exorcism is a very serious business which can be moving and extraordinary. It is used only *in extremis* by the mainline Churches, though some individuals practise it frequently. The film and its attendant publicity have helped to trivialize an important ritual of the Church which should not be abused by being treated as an excuse for another source of supernatural thrills. This is why the Bishop of Exeter also writes: 'The need . . . for the restoration of the practice of exorcism to its proper place is becoming steadily more urgent and more evident'.[4]

1

DEVILS AND DEMONS

The priest, the prophet, the magician, the exorcist. From the moment — buried deep in history — when man began to evolve his own religions and devise his own forms of worship, these roles were mingled. And, in societies where there was a clearly defined concept of good and evil in active opposition to each other, the exorcist was all powerful. He alone could perform the necessary rituals which would expel evil from a person or place and, in doing this, secure good. In some communities the exorcist was so important that he was able to take the credit for cures but also able to disown the failures and impute the blame to others.

Both primitive peoples and those of higher cultural levels were fully aware that the world was filled with an almost limitless horde of spirits, demons and ghosts. But it was not until Christianity became the dominating religion of Europe that the individual figure of Satan himself, Prince of Darkness and overlord of all evil, emerged as a rival to God and almost of the same status. The first hints of such a devil appear in the New Testament and in the Dead Sea Scrolls, but it was several hundred years before he grew in stature and personality until he was able to terrorize almost half the world.

'Satan possesses great courage, incredible cunning, superhuman wisdom, the most acute penetration, consummate prudence, an incomparable skill in veiling the most pernicious artifices under a specious disguise and a malefic and infinite hatred towards the human race.'[1] Such was the view of a distinguished thinker of the sixteenth century.

Modern man, rational and materialistic, may be tempted to laugh at such credulity. But in 1968 an International Gallup Poll revealed that sixty per cent of Americans believed in the devil as an actual individual figure (though invisible) active in the world. There is every reason to think that a similar poll taken today would show an increase in that percentage. C. S. Lewis remarked that the devil is hardly less powerful and much more interesting than God. And though he has been written out of Anglican canon law, Satan it seems will not be put down. Attempts to bind him and his agents through exorcism continue. But he is always ready to pop up again somewhere.

The ability to place responsibility for all evil onto the devil is useful; he becomes a convenient scapegoat. But he is the invention of Christianity, and though other cultures do have quite elaborate demonologies, their legions of spirits were never organized, as it were, under the control of one all-powerful master-spirit setting himself up as the major rival to the predominant god.

Demonology is best described as the scientific study of demons. It is a science which belongs to the past, to the theologians and saints of the middle ages who spent aching hours working out the shapes, sizes and special responsibilities of the various demons that Satan could command. (There was even a demon called Ukobach, who was credited with the invention of fried food!) But the idea of a demonology possibly has its roots in the idea of animism which influenced the attitudes of our primitive ancestors. They believed that all nature was commanded and controlled by invisible spirits upon whose whims all progress relied.

Primitive peoples existed at a basic subsistence level. Without the technology or the sophisticated know-how of an organized civilization, life was a constant struggle with the elements over which men had no control. The unpredictable behaviour of the sea, periods of drought or storm, the appearance of volcanoes and the titanic upheaval of earthquakes were all viewed with awe and fear.

All these phenomena, benevolent or destructive in turn, were gradually seen to be under the control of spirits that had different areas of responsibility — one looked after the sea, another the wind, another the rain, and so on. At the same time primitive man was becoming aware of his soul, a consciousness he built up from dreams and other psychic experiences. The images that came to him he externalized by finding their semblance in nature, in animate and inanimate objects that figured in his own world. In this way primitive man began to visualize the various spirits.

These spirits were equally capable of good or evil. The wind could be smooth and kind, or could appear as a raging hurricane. Rain fertilized crops and made them grow, but its controlling spirit could produce a ruinous deluge, or by witholding its fall produce an even more disastrous drought. The individual spirits had, therefore, to be placated and put into an agreeable frame of mind. Even today the fishermen of the Mediterranean will sometimes pour a glass of wine into the sea to propitiate the sea spirit and prevent a storm.

From these roots the idea of spirits emerged and alongside the concept of worship and sacrifice. Over thousands of years the spirits of nature evolved into those that were exclusively good and those that were entirely harmful. The bad ones were identified as those that inhibit progress and oppose human desires; the good ones were protective and kindly. And so angels and demons were isolated. Eventually the angels merged into the concept of one supreme god and demons became personified into the devil for these primitive peoples.

Evil is relative. For example, to those people who lived in the northern regions of the world, hell was imagined as a place of stunning cold while to those living in the south, hell became a place of fiery heat. In each case those elements that made life most arduous for the people there were magnified in intensity to become hell. Ideas of whàt is evil have varied from culture to culture, but if there is an eternal concept of evil then it is rooted in man's experience of pain and his fear of death. It is in terms of these two fundamental issues that most religions have tried to explain the source of all evil. Since exorcism is one method of attempting to deal with evil, these theories need brief consideration.

Some great religious systems have attributed the creation of the world to one supreme deity who is without any sort of rival with evil power. One of the best examples of such a monotheistic religion is that of ancient Mèsopotamia which comprised the Sumerians, Babylonians and Assyrians, where all diseases and death were attributable to the gods. This is accounted for in their creation myths, in one of which the creators of the world, Enki and Nimmah begin to create freaks, the diseased and malformed purely for fun. Their gods were worshipped and placated with some care and elaboration, and the exorcist was a person of great importance as the extensive demonology had to be kept firmly at bay. The other examples of great monotheistic religions are Judaism, Christianity and Islam.

Then there are the dualistic interpretations of the origin of evil. Here mankind is believed to be involved in a massive struggle between good, creative forces and evil, destructive ones which are in continual opposition. A prime example of this theory is found in Zoroastrianism with its two gods — Ohrmazd who was responsible for good things, and Ahriman who was responsible for the bad ones including poisonous snakes. China has its alternating principles of Yin and Yang (currently receiving a fashionable revival in the West) while the Hindu gods Vishnu and Shiva were equally creators and destroyers of life.

Another variant of dualism is the theory that man consists of an immortal soul imprisoned in a physical body. There is something of this feeling in the poetry of Wordsworth when he writes, 'our birth is but a sleep and a forgetting', and later speaks of 'shades of the prison-house begin to close Upon the growing boy. . .'. The Orphic myth from Greece, Gnosticism and Manicheism are examples of this view.

Originally Judaism was based on a true monotheistic principle with evil, or evil spirits, being agents of God manipulated by him to test or punish his people. However, Judaism eventually absorbed a sort of dualism usually thought to be the result of the exile in Babylonia (about 600 BC) where the influence of the Persian demonologies rubbed off, and the devil with his entourage began to take hold of the imagination. As we shall see in more detail in the next chapter, the devil in the New Testament is held responsible for a wide variety of disease and mental upset as well as being cast as the personal tempter of Christ.

The Bible offers a third interpretation of the source of evil namely that it is due to some prime sin on the part of man himself. This concept is widely known through the Genesis story of Adam and Eve. Having been warned by Yaweh not to eat from the Tree of Knowledge of Good and Evil they nevertheless do, and immediately become aware of their sexuality.

Like many passages in the bible, the story of Adam

and Eve and *the serpent sustains a number of interpretations. Christianity suggests that death and all other
evils are the result of men and women taking part
in the original sin of Adam, with the additional idea
that actual sins committed add to this inherited one,
which is a heavy burden for the devout to bear. It
is important to realize, in the context of Christian
exorcism, that Christianity accounts for the origin of
evil in terms of human sin, past and present.

Christianity also inherited the Judaic concepts of
demons and a devil, along with the appropriate
attitudes to them as revealed in the New Testament.
Also present were certain elements from the mystery
cults that flourished at the time of the decline of
the Roman Empire even though they were regarded
as being entirely creations of the devil along with
the theatres, circuses and fleshly pleasures enjoyed by
the Romans.

Pain and fear of death became associated with the
machinations of the devil; as well as disease, mental
disturbances and curious behaviour, and also many sensual pleasures — a compendium of human sins, prompted
by the malefic agency of the devil and his legion of
demons ever waiting to pounce.

Once Christianity had absorbed the idea of a devil
working in opposition to Christ then he became the
repository of all evils and attempts were made to give
him a history as well as a human physiognomy. Some
theories traced him back to the angel Lucifer, who
had quarrelled with God before the creation and been
ejected from heaven.

*In Genesis the serpent, is not identified with the devil; that was a later
interpretation. It is thought that the presence of the serpent was inspired
by the Mesopotamian Epic of Gilgamesh who was robbed of his chance
of immortality by a serpent.

In defining a devil, Christianity began to create a personage who was to grow to alarming proportions, and who was to wield enormous power. This would mature only several centuries later when the devil became virtually a reality, strong enough to inspire the great witchcraft cult and all its attendant horrors which fell upon the innocent and guilty alike.

As already suggested, it seems to have been a common characteristic of primitive communities to create their demons and ideas of hell from those elements they most feared, or which presented the greatest threat, in their day to day life. It is not surprising to discover therefore, that the demons of the mid-east were always associated with the desert, the terrifying waste spaces that surrounded the tiny centres of population. The ancient Jews had an all-consuming terror of lonely places and of darkness: their deserts were packed with malignant devils and ghouls. Even well into the present century, the orthodox Jew has reserved the right not to be alone in a field, a wide open space or even in an empty house.

The most malevolent of the ancient Jews' demons was Lilith who is mentioned once in the Bible (Isaiah 34.14) where the word is translated as screech owl. Such a bird may not sound too alarming to western ears, but Lilith has a history which puts a different complexion on her appearance. The traditional story has it that when Adam and Eve were cast out of the garden of Eden they were separated, he in Ceylon and she near Mecca, a journey that would take one hundred and seventy five years to make. Lilith presented herself to Adam as a substitute companion, an idea which he appreciated and they enjoyed a happy, loving existence for many years. However, after some time Adam met Eve once more and their original love burst into fresh flame.

Adam rejected Lilith who, furious at the insult, swore to destroy every child of man that should be born. Before Adam died, he divided his estate between the children he had had by Eve. On hearing of this, Lilith brought her offspring by Adam to demand a share, but Adam had, by this time, distributed everything of value to Eve's children. Lilith could have only the deserts and waste places.

The idea that Lilith hovers waiting to destroy children became firmly rooted in the Jewish imagination, and made a contribution to the ceremonies attendant on birth. It is said that one day, the Rabbi Bar-Yechai met Lilith in the desert and attempted a little instant exorcism. He cursed her as evil and demanded that she cease her mischief. In the ensuing dialogue, he discovered that she was afraid of the names of Elijah and of the patriarchs of Israel. So Bar-Yechai prepared a sort of amulet (called a *shmirah*) to act as a protection against her. On the *shmirah* are the names of Shaddai, the Watcher of Israel, Elijah, the names of the patriarchs, the names of the angels Michael and Gabriel, and a hand to drive away evil spirits. It was orthodox tradition to place the *shmirah* on all doors, windows and openings of a house in which a newly born child and its mother lay. This protection lasted for the eight days preceeding circumcision when the child is deemed to have escaped the clutches of Lilith and is admitted into the Covenant of Abraham. (The fate of girl children was of little concern to the Jews).

The legend of Lilith has a certain charm, and it does contain primitive constants that to a certain extent still apply in the handling of demons through exorcism. Most notably finding out from the demon the names it most fears. This is mentioned in the Roman Catholic rubrics on exorcism. Furthermore there is the attribution of natural hazards to demonic intervention — in this case the dangers which must have been attendant on child-birth at that time. Linked into this is the concept of purification rites, the admittance of an individual to a society in the correct way, here symbolized by circum-cision. Exorcism as we understand it was not attempted; Lilith was never bound. Instead those powerful names that made her tremble were used as a defence against her attacks.

The ancient Jews did however absorb from their exile in Babylon the idea of an extended demonology. In the culture of Babylon and Assyria, which had achieved a fairly high level of organization and artistic development, there was an elaborate gallery of demons which included jinn, ghouls, vampires, malignant disembodied ghosts and terrifying hordes of hostile spirits that would stream in from the deserts. A sophisticated and ordered demon-ology seems a natural concomitant with a society's move upwards from a subsistence economy. Demons, instead of representing the weather and other hostile elements become associated with anything that threatens the new *status quo* — basic systems of organization, or the social order itself. It could be the subversion of established moral codes as well as the very personal things which man always fears — death, disease, deformity.

It is often said that the devil belongs to the East, and certainly the ancient Babylonians decided that there were enough demons to contend with in their world. They lurked in graves, on mountains, in caves and among the marshes. They were able to enter cities too, creeping silently along the streets, sliding through door-ways, riding in on the fierce desert winds. One such was Pazuzu, demon wind and bringer of disease and used as the leitmotiv of Blatty's book *The Exorcist*.

A whole army of demons haunted the Assyrian deserts

and was said to be comprised of 'warriors, destroyers, vampires, phantoms, and ghosts'. One story has it that they were so dreadful that when shown their own reflections in giant mirrors the demons themselves fled in terror. Another story holds that gigantic pictures of the demons were painted on city walls, which also had the effect of scaring them away.

It was in this atmosphere that the exorcist became popular and powerful. He was in constant demand, needed to confront victims of disease, to assist at the consecration of temples, at burials and the various seasonal ceremonies; on any occasion, in fact, that might be assumed to attract the attention of the destructive demons. Cuneiform texts from the middle of the third millenium B.C. reveal many forms of exorcism, incantations and prayers used to cast out devils and the ghosts of the dead.

When man began to order his life he became increasingly aware of the disorder in the universe, and this disunity is probably one of the major achievements of the devil. The elaboration of magic rites becomes a kind of system of equilibrium, an attempt to impose order. A sense of this factor contributed to the importance of the exorcist.

Naturally enough, exorcisms were carried out in the names of the ruling gods, notably Ea who was the Lord of Wisdom and ruler of the healing waters. Waters were used to invoke the gods and the exorcism rites consisted of carefully cast litanies calling upon Marduk, Ea's son, to intercede. They ended with the incantation: 'By Heaven be ye exorcized! By earth be ye exorcized'. The name of the deity had to be invoked and it was also important to call out the demon by his name. Since there were hundreds of individual demons, all with names, the exorcist was more or less forced to recite them all so that he could be sure of mentioning the demon responsible for the particular condition with which he was dealing.

Discovering the name of the demon has always been an important factor in all forms of exorcism. When at war, the early Romans would conduct a ritual of calling out the gods of the opposing army before they attacked an enemy town. These gods were invited to join Rome, and were promised all kinds of worship and good treatment if they did so. This ritual — called an *evocatio* — was demoralizing for the enemy. However, it was of vital importance that the correct names of the gods were used. The Romans themselves, fearful that an enemy should similarly try to invoke their gods, always concealed the name of the guardian spirit of Rome. The writers Servius and Pliny state that it was not known whether this guardian spirit was, in fact, male or female.

Rituals accompanied incantations. The patient was sprinkled with water which it was believed, would drive out the evil influence and absorb it into itself. Perfumes would be used and also flour which would be scattered around the person — possibly a fertility-creativity symbol. Sometimes a black and white yam would be fastened to the individual's bed while the exorcist held, during the ritual, a branch of the sacred tamarisk. Animals sometimes appeared, as sacrifices or as scapegoats to aid the transference of the contagion and the exorcist was also able to remove the evil and place it in seven loaves of pure dough, which were carried into the desert.

It is interesting to note that much later, in the fourth century A.D., Cyril of Jerusalem in his sermons designed to help the pagans who had been converted to Christianity, specifically refers to offerings of dough and to the habit of burning incense by healing waters to effect a cure, as being deceits of the devil and objectionable to the new faith. Clearly, the influence of these ancient

Babylonic exorcism rites was strong and pervasive. Eridu, the seat of worship of Ea and Marduk, was held in reverence in ancient Babylonia and was the original centre for exorcism rites. The methodology developed there certainly became the predominant form used, with minor local variations, throughout the mid-east.

A similar situation prevailed in ancient Egypt. There existed no separate function of exorcism or similar office. But the defence against possible evil and the expulsion of discovered evil were a prime responsibility of the *sunu*, or doctor-priest. This charismatic figure was able to control supernatural powers, particularly the work of the gods of healing on one hand and the disruptive efforts of the demons of disease on the other.

Once more we find a familiar pattern of incantation allied to ritual with the additional requirement here that the correct day, and even the precise time of that day had to be ascertained before the ceremony could be undertaken. Again it was important to secure the name of the indwelling demon and to expel it in the name of the presiding deity. 'It is Isis who says it.' Or, Re or Horus, as the case might be. The exorcist used his own discrimination as to whether or not to invoke the relevant god, to pretend to be the god himself or to rely on magical arts he had used successfully before.

Very little information has survived from this period, but there are ancient texts which describe in some detail certain rituals particularly those relating to bites from snakes and other dangerous reptiles which would be a major hazard in Egypt. The young sun-god Horus was always invoked in this context. Contemporary carvings of Horus illustrate him standing on crocodiles and holding in his hands, snakes and scorpions.

The exorcist-physician would recite an incantation over either a hawk made of isy-wood with two feathers

in its head, or over a sacred stela on which was written
the story of Isis and Horus, in itself a holy object. The
form of incantation seems to have been devised as much
to promote courage in the patient as to invoke the god
and defeat the demon. One would hardly expect the
exorcist to have a hundred per cent success with it:

> Flow out thou poison, come forth upon the ground.
> Horus conjures thee, cuts thee off, splits thee out,
> and thou risest not up but fallest down. Thou art
> weak and not strong, a coward and dost not fight,
> blind and dost not see. Thou liftest not thy face.
> Thou art turned back and findest not thy way. Thou
> mournest and does not rejoice. Thou creepest away
> and dost not appear. So speaketh Horus, efficacious
> of magic![2]

The wooden hawk would then be brushed against the
sufferer's face. Water would be poured over the stela,
making it holy, which would then be employed in the
mixing of medicine. Beer, bread and incense also took
their places in the ritual.

In these ancient civilizations the function of exorcism
was different from that developed later by the Christian
church even though externally the various rites and
prayers seem to have a superficial similarity. An incantation accompanied by a sprinkling of water in the name of
Ea or Horus seems not so very different from a prayer
accompanied by a sprinkling of holy water in the name
of Christ.

Christianity on becoming the official religion of Rome
gained its strength through force of law as much as anything but was nevertheless impelled by a strong evange-
listic fervour. The pagan religions were, on the whole,
fairly tolerant of each other and while certain cults
spread throughout the mid-east and the Mediterranean

B

coasts, many different forms of worship existed amicably side by side with a sort of implicit acknowledgement that what was appropriate for Assyria was not perhaps, suitable for Egypt.

To the Christian, however, anything outside the true faith with its one god, was dubbed automatically the product of the devil. So exorcism though it was used for healing purposes in the pattern set by Christ was also a means of spreading the boundaries of Christ's kingdom through remarkable initiation ceremonies which would instill the new adherents with what literally amounted to holy terror.

In pagan religions then, exorcism was used primarily for the healing of sickness (which was seen as the result of demonic attack) and also as an aid to the imposition of a sense of order onto a disturbing world. Certainly it was essential, as in Christian exorcism, for the expelled evil to be replaced by good, but the rite was not used as a means of extending the worship of the local deity. If this was to be done then it would be achieved through warfare, the capture and oppression of the defeated.

Exorcism was specifically a branch of the healing arts and the exorcist worked alongside the person we would recognize as a physician or surgeon or, as in Egypt, he himself would be the doctor. If there was a division of labour then the doctor attended to the physical symptoms, the exorcist to the demonic causation, thus aligning himself with the duties of the priest. In the case of failure, the doctor would be the person blamed.

The advanced and influential cultures of Greece and Rome did not possess a separate class of exorcists, and those rites that could be associated with the principle as such were much more certainly classified as healing or purification ceremonies. By the fifth century B.C. for example, the cult of Asklepios was established in Greece, and Epidaurus had become the centre of healing with a reputation something similar to that of Lourdes today. The main healing method used was what is called incubation — that is, the sick person slept in the temple and during the night was vouchsafed mystical dreams or visions which were possibly promoted by the suggestive ceremonies of the priests, and which brought about relief or a cure.

Purification ceremonies featured strongly in the religious practices of ancient Rome. These peoples, though urbanized, retained a somewhat animistic view of nature, regarding some spirits as hostile, others as beneficial. Purification processions were conducted around their fields and settlements to expel any evil that might be lurking there.

During the well-known Lupercalia, which celebrated the founding of Rome by Romulus and Remus, naked youths would run around the Palatine hill flourishing thongs made from the hide of goats with which they would strike bystanders, thus forming a protective magic circle. It was also believed that women who were struck by the Luperci would be cured of barrenness. These rituals then, certainly had some connection with fertility ceremonies as well. Generally speaking though, the Romans did not develop a demonology. Indeed they were not inclined to see either divine inspiration, or anti-social manifestations of whatever order, in terms of charismatic spirit possession.

By firmly relegating all non-Christian forms of worship to the domain of the devil, and by attributing all forms of personal conduct that did not find favour with the Christian ethic to the work of the devil, Christianity very quickly allowed itself the thin end of the wedge of dualism. Signs that the devil was going to emerge as a

distinct personality are first seen from his appearance as
the tempter of Christ, an episode that has an almost
fairy-story quality as the Good Prince and the Bad Prince
stand chatting on a mountain top about the possibilities
of inheritance.

In the New Testament, it might be argued that the
devil may be a mere symbol of worldly temptation, representing the thoughts of ambition and power. But by
the third century A.D. there were signs that he was becoming an even bigger and more rounded personality,
controlling much more than inner human values. And in
the fifteenth century he had evolved as a single, formidable character, controlling hundreds if not millions of
nasty little demons, and setting himself up as the equal
of, and in opposition to, God.

This poses another important distinction between the
Christian devil and the demons of other religions or
systems of belief. For the Christian devil is, in the imagination of those who have tried to portray him since
medieval times, uniquely human. It is probable that re-
presentations of the devil exceed in number those of
Christ, while God tends to remain immune to pictorial
delineation, at the most a luminous and benevolent
figure throned in pink clouds.

Every culture, has created its own images of devils and
demons out of its own particular fears and hates. The
animism that informs the outlook of primitive tribes
still survives for us to see today in such pictures. The
Eskimo produces wooden masks, carvings of primeval
force and beauty. A hideous, snarling face has, super-
imposed upon it, the graceful curved shape of the salmon,
an artefact representing at once the fish and the demon
that lurks within it. The fantastical, semi-human, quasi-
bestial images of pre-Colombian America have been continued through the centuries as a living reality, fixed to

the totem poles and hanging protectively as guardians of settlements for the people of the plains.

Inhabitants of countries that have at least a veneer of civilization retain their charms and amulets as protective devices against animals and elements, and the wicked charms of others who may be their enemies. Roman Catholic countries like South America still feel an inner recall to the magic of the jungle, to spiritism and a real understanding of the demons of the animal world.

As we have seen, in many cultures, the gods represent order. The demons are responsible for those happenings which disrupt or contest that order; not a moral order so much as the evils of pain, plague and famine, attendants of death. If correctly invoked the gods will exorcize these demons. The Christian inheritance consists first of these demons of the desert which, visually, have an animal diabolism. Tiamat the Babylonian devil of chaos was a horned and clawed fowl; Lilith, we have seen, was a screech owl; Set, the Egyptian god of chaos, was depicted as a snake or a crocodile. Tusks, horns, protruding tongues, spiked tails, talons, clawed feet, fiery breath — all adorn the fearful idols and carvings; all the antithesis of beauty and of order. In *The Exorcist* Blatty described the demon Pazuzu who was the demon of the southwest wind, bringing fever and delirium: 'Ragged wings, talonned feet, bulbous, jutting, stubby penis and a mouth stretched taut in feral grin.' Pazuzu appears in carvings and a bronze statuette of him exists.

This demon, who appears as late as the seventh century, is a particularly relevant creature in this context, for in him we find incorporated the most familiar features of the Judeo-Christian devil who still stares at us from the gargoyles, the capitals and screens, and the illuminated manuscripts of medieval Europe. Christianity absorbed the plastic imagination and artistic inheritance of the

Greeks and began to realize in visual terms a devil drawn from the Assyrian deserts.

But Christianity spread westwards and northwards; it looked away from the burning sun and pestilence-ridden deserts and conquered the gentler climates, the softer wooded and pastoral lands of Europe moving towards the bleaker and colder environment of the north. And slowly the devil acquired a new body, designed for him out of elements in the religious cultures that were absorbed or outlawed by the new faith. It is important to realize that these various cults and pagan forms of worship were by no means demonic *per se*, but Christianity was determined to make them so.

This method of absorbing other cults and grafting their symbolism onto a Christian conception of the devil has given rise to many misapprehensions and misconceptions about the nature of witchcraft through the ages, culminating in the assumption that witchcraft equates with Satanism, which is certainly not so. The two things are quite different in a fundamental way. Certainly indiscriminate condemnation by the Church and the popular imagination and the confusion of some commentators have all helped to make the two seem indistinguishable. But the religion known as witchcraft is generally recognized as pre-dating Christianity and as such had no devil to worship. Nor could rites that were in existence before the Christian Church came along be possibly interpreted as a perversion or a blasphemy on that Church.

Possibly the first representation of some kind of image — demon or deity, perhaps a bit of both — known in the world appears among the wall carvings of the paleolithic caves in southern France. They are shadowy, meagre figures but all have the enduring characteristic of being horned. Where this fundamental image comes from no one really knows. It may be quite simply that beasts with horns represented to the paleolithic huntsmen the most threatening aspects of their world. Others have offered more complex theories, not the least interesting being that there is a race-memory of some pre-historic invasion of horned monsters from outer space!

Be that as it may, the horned god occurs constantly through the ages, known as the god of the Witches, it is always associated with fertility and pagan cults in the rural countryside. Most familiarly this horned god appears as Pan, the Roman figure associated with woodlands, adorned with horns and hooves, enticing and able to create a form of mass possession among his followers. In England the horned god occurs in various forms connected with the old, or pre-Christian religion. Famously he appears as Herne the Hunter, the spectral figure who was supposed to haunt Windsor Great Park, ancient and distant enough to be used by Shakespeare for a few laughs in *The Merry Wives of Windsor*. Most prominently the horned god represents fertility and enjoyable sexual love governed by individual or group morality rather than by one imposed from outside.

Such an attitude to sex was anathema to the Christian morality. The horn of the horned god was certainly a fertility symbol and had nothing to do with the devil. It was adopted as a satanic symbol of the oppressive attitudes towards sex. What was originally a sign of creativity and spontaneity became distorted into a symbol of repression and, as we shall see, sexual repression was to be a significant element in what later came to be known as demonic possession.

As Christianity became established and matured, the devil rode out in a big way. The number of demons grew and grew until one particularly dedicated demonologist managed to isolate 7,405,926 of them divided into elaborate hierarchies and classes and organized to be responsible for every possible aspect of human suffering. The contemporary American Satanist with his list of 86, seems a mere novice and some of his seem of a fairly minor nature, such as Phoenix who speaks in parables and Vepar who inflicts worms. Hagenti who turns wine into water may not be popular, nor Agares who causes earthquakes.

In the sixteenth century, however, such demonologies were part and parcel of universal belief. One may assume that there must have been at least some theologians or intellectuals who realized how absurd the whole thing was becoming. But it was an age of uncertainty and social disruption, and the demonologists exacerbated the general feelings of anxiety, whether consciously or unconsciously one cannot ascertain.

As we shall see in a later chapter, literally thousands of individuals were driven mad and it has been estimated that between 1450 and 1750 some three million people in Europe and colonial America were executed for Satanic involvement. The devil was a reality; strange animals, misshapen human beings, even ordinary domestic creatures could be dubbed, feared, and perhaps slaughtered as devils in disguise.

The tripping verse of a fourteenth century miracle play, *The Passion of St Quentin* indicates the range of devils that were available to the popular imagination.

> Smooth devils, Horned devils
> Sullen Devils, Playful Devils,
> Shorn Devils, Hairy Devils,
> Foolish Devils,
> Devils, Devilesses, and Young Devils . . .

In what is recognized as a manner typical of the English, the devil was, for a certain time, ridiculed and made fun of through the medium of the mystery plays that were performed on the great festival days and in which were enacted stories from the Bible in the great squares outside the cathedrals. The English have a habit of making fun of things they fear and the villains of the mystery plays — Herod, Beelzebub — were transformed into rip-roaring crowd-pleasers, the devil emerging with his comedy cauldron and comical long spoon.

There have been fashions in devils, as in everything else. When Tertullian called the devil 'God's ape', Satan was then drawn in that shape. In an age of puritanism when anything alluring was automatically suspect, then the devil could be beautiful — an enticing woman for the male chauvinist society. In the north the devil was given a limp like Wotan; elsewhere his face would appear black and wrinkled, or with a beard. Slowly he accumulated a positively theatrical wardrobe of costumes and make-ups.

A description of Satan today would contain certain constants that are non-human: the horns, the cloven hoof, the tail and possibly wings. But these are simply accessories to a humanoid figure. The influence of the romantic imagination with its Gothic fantasies of vampires and Satanic masses (a vision supported with the technicolor glamour of the movie industry) will give this figure a certain magnetism which is far from offensive. The clothes will be black (a medieval conceit) and will be of romantic sweep with vampiric cloak and operatic tights maybe. He will have penetrating, luminous eyes, a leer or grin, a beard trimmed to a point. The eyes and ears will slant slightly upwards — interesting rather than grotesque. He will, above all, vibrate with a sexuality that gives a frisson to the sadist and the masochist alike.

This is a devil fit for a time when almost everything that was once firmly attributed to diabolic intervention — from scrofula to war — has either been explained or rationalized into a political necessity. All Satan has left to manipulate are deviations from a certain strict moral code: the guilt of luxury, the delights of sexual licence, the excitement of gambling, the thrill of breaking another social taboo. He has moved a long way from Pazuzu.

To the Christian, this devil and his demons are objects that must of course be repelled. A great deal of energy was spent finding out means of expelling them from the human body, less in deciding how they entered in the first place. From its status as a part — but a vital part — of initiation and baptism, exorcism rose to be a unique and essential ritual based on the practical example of Christ.

2

CHRIST THE EXORCIST

> . . . God anointed Jesus of Nazareth with the Holy
> Ghost and with power: who went about doing good, and
> healing all that were oppressed of the devil; for God
> was with him.
>
> Acts 10. 38

The statement is clear and unequivocal. It is made by the apostle Peter during his sermon at Caesarea, and it emphasizes that the ability to release men from the power of the devil was central to the ministry of Christ. All the early preachers underscored this function as they spread the word of Christ, using it as powerful evidence to assert the authenticity of Christ as the messenger of God. The claim was a literal one and had ample foundation: in the synoptic gospels demoniacs are presented as the most frequent objects of Christ's curative powers.

In the Gospel According to St John, the first miracle that Christ performs after his return to Galilee from his baptism is the conversion of water into wine. Mark and Luke, however, present a simple but highly dramatic exorcism as the first practical, public demonstration of the powers of Christ.

At this stage in his career, Christ was not regarded as the Messiah. He was, to all intents and purposes, the son of Joseph of Nazareth and, as such, was something of a local curiosity. His preaching was far more impactive than anything the people of Galilee had previously experienced, being creative and dynamic rather than a weary repetition of familiar dogmas: 'He taught them as one that had authority, not as the scribes'.

On this particular occasion Christ had been teaching in the synagogue at Capernaum and had astonished the congregation with his words. Among those present was a man possessed by an unclean spirit. This man rushes out of the crowd to confront Christ, challenging him using the voice and the character of the demon that inhabits him: 'Leave us alone: what have we to do with thee, thou Jesus of Nazareth? Art thou come to destroy us? I know thee who thou art, the Holy One of God.' Immediately Christ turns and replies angrily: 'Hold thy peace, and come out of him!' Christ is, it is important to realize, speaking directly to the demon, not to the man himself.

According to Mark, the unclean spirit tears the man, cries out in a loud voice and then leaves him. Luke tells us that the devil throws the man down before quitting his body. Both descriptions suggest a convulsive fit, the man rolling and crying in agony as his possessive demon is exorcized, then quite possibly lapsing into a coma or faint. This impressive and apparently successful exorcism has a tremendous effect on the bystanders who are awed by the power and authority of this young man who 'commands the unclean spirits and they come out'.

Such a concept — of Christ as exorcist — is not, perhaps, readily appreciated by the modern mind. The image of Christ has been popularly presented in many ways: as a milk-and-water figure trailing mists of Victorian sentiment; as a rather distant intellectual; as a small town revolutionary. But his function as exorcist has never been particularly emphasized.

Perhaps to do so might have been considered lending him the suspect status of wizard in a world that increasingly demands rationality. And indeed, while exorcism has become so closely associated with the spurious and often sensational trappings of magic and the occult, to make a link between the mission of Christ and what has come to be regarded as a remnant of medieval superstition may certainly seem inappropriate.

And yet this was one of the major means by which Christ polarized concepts of good and evil — in visible, dramatic terms instantly comprehensible to the people among whom he moved. He made a firm articulation of the tension between God and the devil, and subsequently exorcism and possession became concrete facts in Christianity. As the early Church developed, exorcism rituals were an integral part of the initiation ceremonies for neophytes to the Christian mysteries. The mystagogs, such as St John Chrysostom and Theodore of Mopsuestia carefully elaborated them into their baptismal homilies.

These ritualistic passages were not intended to be used for cases of individual possession. Taking the cue from Christ's assertion that those who were not for him were against him, it was taken for granted that non-Christians must inevitably be contaminated by devilish influences that had to be exorcized before admittance to the Church.

While the Christian Church was in an embattled position, defining its role in contention with the forces of evil personified in witchcraft and Satanic cults, (in fact genuinely alternative religions, converting their adherents) then the exorcism rituals remained — both those formulated to deal with specific cases of possession and those incorporated into initiation ceremonies.

Later the ceremonies fell into disuse, the lengthy initiation exorcism routines were reduced to a brief acknowledgement in the regular service of baptism, and individual exorcisms became rare. And, of course, Christ's own role as a highly practical exorcist tended to be subsumed into his more general and acceptable role of miracle worker and healer.

There is a further relevant reason why this fundamental aspect of Christ's earthly work should have received scant attention. The rapid increase of knowledge about the physical nature of illness and the functioning of the body has cast doubts upon the literal interpretations of Christ's exorcisms; and a closer understanding of mental and psychosomatic illness has prompted further reappraisals. There are three or four examples of Christ's powers as exorcist in the gospels which, through their drama, are particularly well-known: the demoniac at Capernaum already mentioned, the episode of the Gadarene swine and that of the woman bent double by Satan. But there were many others who were dealt with by Christ or by his disciples. Sometimes it seems that just about anyone who was not complete in body and healthy in mind was assumed to be possessed, and to modern eyes, the types of cases that confronted Christ appear to be victims, not of demons, but of various illnesses. Diagnoses of these illnesses today would probably include epilepsy, schizophrenia, arthritis and manic depression. And they would be offered the relevant medical or psychiatric treatments.

This perspective places the interpreter of the gospels in a difficult position. If he wishes to promote their literal, documentary accuracy, then he must claim that all illness is of demonic or even Satanic origin, today as well as then. Or he must argue that symptoms which today have a physical or mental causation had, two thousand years ago, a spiritual one. Both ideas are clearly untenable; the first fights with scientific information, the second is simply illogical.

Theologians and scholars have debated these points at length over the years, examining the translations, testing the exact meanings of the original Greek words and studying in mind the contemporary cultural context. For example, it has been suggested that the reason John does not mention demoniacs or exorcism in his gospel was because the cultivated Greeks of Asia Minor would have found such things incredible or offensive. John is believed to have written for this audience and omitted the demoniac cures to accord with its ideas. Generally, two broad ways out of the manifold difficulties of matching the exorcism stories with modern knowledge have been developed, each using what is called an accommodation theory.

One theory suggests that while Christ himself certainly possessed divine healing powers, he was aware that demonic possession was not the actual cause of the illnesses that were rife in the land. What he did was to accommodate his words and actions to accord with the popular beliefs or superstitions of the time. Throughout history, and the present time is no exception, popular leaders have not hesitated to use the expediency of speaking in the language best understood by those they wish to influence.

A second theory accepts that Christ, and everyone else, including the authors of the synoptic gospels, believed in demonic possession as a cause of illness and consequently in exorcism as a cure. We, however, know better and must therefore interpret the synoptists accounts of the incidents as allegories rather than as literal happenings. An example of this is the story of the Gadarene swine, which is frequently used as a parable, or image, of hysteria communicating itself to others and leading to an orgy of mass self-destruction. This is a favourite image of the opponents of any movement in society which significantly perhaps, appears to be in contradiction to the tenets of Christianity itself.

In the gospel narrative, a possessed man is exorcized by Christ and the expelled demons are rehoused in a herd of swine which instantly plunge over a cliff into the sea. Figuratively it is a powerful image indeed: the message is that evil (whether it is Communism, abortion, the abolition of censorship or the legalization of marijuana) is fascinating, highly infectious and destructive.

This seems to have been the way (in the language of social imagery) that the more problematic exorcisms of Christ have been presented. And certainly in many instances, the words of Christ immediately after an exorcism do seem to imply a moral statement about the human condition generally, still applicable today. For example, when Christ is accused of using the devil to cast out the devil, he replies in the subsequent argument that a house divided against itself will fall.

It would seem therefore, that there is every justification for reading the texts in this way, but it still leaves the actual veracity of the exorcisms and the validity of possession in doubt. And Fr J. H. Crehan S.J., a leading expert on exorcism, writes: 'One cannot dismiss the New Testament exorcisms as so much hysteria'.[1] In other words, they deserve to be taken seriously and, more than that, have significant messages about the existence of Satan, the power of evil, and the powers of redemption.

A great deal has been allowed to stand between the reader and the realities of the New Testament, of which the suggestion that incidents involving demonic possession should be read as metaphors is one. The extrapolation of pious texts, the sentimental Sunday School approach, even the intellectual exegeses of scholars have all conspired to obscure the dynamic reportage character of the gospels. The image of a mild and gentle Jesus is not easily displaced from the consciousness. Yet meekness and mildness are of little help when one confronts a person in the grip of demonic possession. And Christ, as we shall see, employed a very powerful form of vocal conjuration to expel demons.

Before looking in more detail at some notable examples of Christ's exorcisms, it may be useful to make a few general points about the attitudes and expectations of his contemporaries regarding the devil and demons. The basic notion that evil spirits could influence men was prevalent among the Hebrews, and it was recognized that such spirits could cause undesirable physical effects upon those visited. They might manifest themselves as a physical illness, such as epilepsy or as a mental disturbance, such as depression. The melancholy of Saul, for example, was attributed to 'the evil spirit from God' (1 Samuel 18.10). At this time it was believed that God controlled all spirits, good and evil, as his agents. There are no accounts of exorcisms in the Old Testament, though the Genesis Apocryphon does include a passage describing how Abraham exorcized the Egyptian Pharaoh.

The concept of Satan as a separate entity did not emerge until after the destruction of the Hebrew state by Nebuchadnezzar. And Satan, with his entourage of evil spirits became an autonomous and active force for evil in direct opposition to God and his angels. It was not until about 500 B.C. that the even more distinct idea was formulated that evil spirits (from Satan's court) could actually enter the body and take possession of its members. This development is attributed to the influence of the theory of spiritual beings that spread from the orient, particularly from the ruling Persians with their Zend mythology and its wicked Deves that existed before the human race. Accordingly, the Hebrews would

understand their devils to be the souls of the wicked
people who existed before the flood as well as the
fallen angels of Genesis.

This now recognized possibility of individual possession implies the possibility of individual exorcism, and
later Jewish writings do include accounts of exorcisms.
One author, the historian Josephus, suggests that God
taught the art of exorcism to Solomon. There are, in
fact, quite a number of legends attached to Solomon.
In one he is credited with binding the seventy-two rulers
of evil spirits in a brass jar which was then thrown into
the sea. Some generations later the jar was washed up
and the demon princes allowed to escape. But there
are, no references to these exploits of Solomon in the
Old Testament.[2]

The apocryphal *Testaments of the Twelve Patriarchs*
also present a background that includes established
practices for the expulsion of demons. The *Testament
of Ruben* tells us that the spirit of deceit sends seven
other spirits upon a man: lust, gluttony, anger, flattery,
pride, lying and grasping at injustice. This sounds like a
recitation of the traditional seven deadly sins, but the
idea of seven other spirits is found more than once in
the gospels. Seven devils, for example, were cast out
of Mary called Magdalene, and Christ, in one of his
lectures, refers to the idea that an expelled demon will
return 'seven other spirits more wicked than himself'.

Methods of exorcism were principally conjuration
used in conjunction with certain stones and amulets,
and also fumigations such as incense, of which the
Hebrews had a great traditional knowledge, supposed
to have been handed down from Solomon. It is
interesting to remember at this point that frankincense
and myrrh were offered at the nativity, both materials
used in exorcism rites at this time.

Christ was born into a world where the practice of exorcism was familiar. And one may wonder, just how successful these exorcists were. Certainly Christ does imply at one point that some were successful ('If I by Beelzebub cast out devils, by whom do your children cast them out . . . ?'). Nevertheless it is abundantly clear that a great deal of Christ's impact among the people lay in the demonstration that his exorcisms actually worked: 'And all the people were amazed and said, "Is not this the son of David?" ' This must imply that others were not so successful.

The Jewish exorcists that Paul meets in Ephesus were already in practice and are described as vagabonds, suggesting perhaps that the exorcist occupied a status similar to that of the wandering soothsayer or quack doctor of later centuries. That these Ephesian exorcists were swift to adopt the name of Jesus in their rituals, recognizing it as a name more powerful than that which they had been using, suggests a kind of opportunism.

And on another occasion, the disciple John reports back to Jesus that he had encountered an exorcist casting out devils and using Christ's name to do it. 'But we forbad him, because he followeth not us.' In modern terms this sounds suspiciously like someone cashing in on another's success. It is evident, therefore, that exorcisms were familiar, that Christ therefore was not doing something unusual but that his success was impressive and that others attempted to imitate his style.

Against this background, the importance of the New Testament exorcisms begins to emerge. The power of an exorcist would be expected of the Messiah, just as a particular pattern of miracles as predicted in the Old Testament would be expected. And by his actions Christ may be seen to be formulating concrete concepts. Of defining evil, or wickedness on the one hand, and on the other, marking out the path to redemption and the remission of sins. 'Be sober, be vigilant; because your adversary the devil, as a roaring lion, walketh about, seeking whom he may devour' writes Peter in just one of many examples of this new vision of life.

Christ's first exorcism — that of the demoniac in the synagogue at Capernaum — has been described. Perhaps even more vividly dramatic is Christ's encounter with the demoniac in the country of the Gadarenes. This is narrated in all three synoptic gospels, and each version contains some significant differences which have considerably exercised the minds of interpreters.

Matthew's account is the briefest and the least detailed. Christ and the disciples have crossed the sea of Galilee to its eastern side; it was a stormy passage and during it Christ performed his nature miracle of calming the wind and the waves. They land at Gadarenes and on this desolate shore, Christ is confronted by two men, possessed of devils. These men live in the tombs and are described as being so fierce that they have always prevented anyone from passing through the place. As with the demoniac at Capernaum, the possessed men react immediately to the presence of Christ, crying out — in the personae of the demons: 'What have we to do with thee, Jesus, thou Son of God? art thou come hither to torment us before the time?' Matthew does not record any answer to this challenge, but as the demons continue by beseeching Christ that if he is going to cast them out, to cast them into the herd of swine grazing nearby. Jesus says, Merely, 'Go!' and the devils leave the men, enter the herd which then runs down a steep slope into the sea. Everyone is suitably amazed and the swineherds rush off to the city to report the event. The citizens emerge and ask Christ to leave the area, which he does without further comment.

Compared with the accounts of Mark and Luke, this one is puzzling in its brevity and lack of further detail. The Gadarene exorcism is a frightening episode, and certainly was one of considerable importance, not least because of its extreme difficulty. This becomes apparent when one considers the other versions.

The situation is the same: a stormy crossing of the Sea of Galilee, a landing followed by direct confrontation with the demoniac. Mark and Luke, however, introduce just one possessed man, not two. And they describe him in considerable detail. Luke informs us that he was naked; Mark offers the information that he had often been bound with chains, but that he was always able to tear them apart and was, moreover, beyond the control of men. Luke tells us, too, that the possessed man wandered, day and night, among the mountains, crying out and slashing himself with stones. The appearance of the man must, therefore, have been fearful — naked, bleeding, howling and with enormous strength.

All the writers agree that he lived in the tombs. These would be rooms cut out of rocks, or the earth, and used to house those with whom it was intolerable to live in the city — lepers and those considered insane or demoniacally possessed.

Mark and Luke also introduce the presence of a herd of swine, with their keepers, grazing nearby. Mark says there were about two thousand swine; Luke just says there were 'many swine'. The scene comes eerily to life: a wild, deserted shore; a tormented man; the proximity of beasts traditionally regarded as brutish.

Commentators have exercised themselves over the actual progress of the ensuing dialogue. But it really seems to have been a straightforward question and answer, with the demoniac instantly recognizing the

Messiah and the demons within him reacting accordingly: 'What have I to do with thee, Jesus, thou Son of the most high God?'

Jesus then commands: 'Come out of the man, thou unclean spirit'.

The demon replies: 'I adjure thee by God, that thou torment me not'.

Christ then asks: 'What is thy name?'

'My name is Legion: for we are many', the demons reply. But the demons seem to realize they are to be expelled because they now beseech Jesus not to send them out of the country (Mark) or into the sea (Luke) and they request to be sent into the herd of swine. Jesus agrees to this and the demons leave the man and apparently enter the swine for at once the entire herd stampedes over the cliff into the water, where all the swine drown.

The swineherds then rush away to the city to recount this dramatic event and when the people arrive to gaze at Jesus they also find the possessed man now restored to his right mind, clothed and cleaned up, sitting with him. The populace is awed to the extent that they ask Jesus to leave. The now exorcized man begs Jesus to take him along but Jesus refuses, telling him to go back home to his friends and family, and to inform them how he came to be cured 'and show how great things the Lord hath done for thee'.

Aspects of this story that have particularly puzzled later commentators are the questions of whether it is possible for one individual to be possessed by more than one demon at a time, and why the demons, having chosen to be rehoused in a herd of swine, should then promptly proceed to kill their new host-bodies.

The first is regarded as evidence to support the extreme difficulty of this particular exorcism. Most of the other New Testament exorcisms involve the expulsion of one demon from one individual. And these individuals are shown as living without harassment from their condition, among their friends and families. The Gadarene demoniac is particularly shown as being in a dreadful physical condition, and moreover, as having been rejected by society, abandoned and forced to live in a sort of compound outside the city.

Some commentators have seriously pontificated that it is inconceivable for several demons to set up habitation in one person. But if one believes in the reality of demons and in possession, it does seem somewhat arbitrary to begin inventing rules as to what they can and cannot do. Moreover, it is well known that people who are regarded as mad may assume different characteristics within a short space of time (violence, hysterical outbursts, laughter, weeping, etc.) and is an accepted form for portraying madness in drama. If Ophelia, for example, was regarded as being possessed, then her auditors would discern more than one personality emergent in her various ravings, and would be justified in assuming she was possessed of several demons. One must also remember that the concept of seven demons inhabiting one person is mentioned in the New Testament (in reference to Mary Magdalene) and in contemporary writings. Although, of course, a Roman Legion consisted of more than seven soldiers, it is agreed that the demons described themselves as Legion in order to impress with a reference to what must have been a common enough sight.

It is likely then that the Gadarene is described as being possessed by a Legion of demons in order to emphasize the extreme difficulty of the case. It cannot be insignificant, either, that Christ suffered a rough sea crossing to perform this feat and then simply to return. Clearly his journey must have had an important reason.

The mass suicide of the swine might well belong to the same category of dramatic colouration, inserted as a circumstantial incident to indicate that the demons really had departed. At that period a physical demonstration was sometimes required to prove the success of an exorcism — the departing demon was required to overturn a statue or to tip over a vessel of water. Certainly this brings exorcism down to the level of mere conjuring, for surely the greatest proof of its success must ultimately lie in the subsequent behaviour of the exorcized person. And the Gadarene is unmistakably described as not just being back in his right mind, but clothed and — by implication — cleaned up.

The Gadarene exorcism is certainly the most sensational of the many described, or referred to in passing, by the gospel writers. As I remarked earlier, it sometimes seems as though anyone who was sick in body or mind would be regarded as possessed. But this is not really so. There was certainly a wide variety of sickness and disease prevalent at that time and doctors were not completely ignorant and could recognize different symptoms. Many Jewish dietary and social laws, too, can be found to have a realistic basis in simple hygiene and some contemporary beliefs, particularly relating to food, centered around the transmission of disease: not picking up scraps of food, or drinking someone else's water, washing of hands and fasting were regarded as precautions against possession.

Matthew includes a general description of the sort of cures done by Christ and makes the categories quite clear. 'And they brought unto him all sick people that were taken with divers diseases and torments, and those which were possessed with devils, and those which were lunatics, and those that had the palsy; and he

healed them.' Here possession is firmly separated from
ordinary illness, lunacy and paralysis. Later, however,
when narrating exorcisms Matthew seems to contradict
himself. A father brings his lunatic son for a cure: 'Lord,
have mercy on my son: for he is lunatic and sore vexed:
for oft times he falleth into the fire, and oft into the
water'. Jesus rebukes the devil which leaves the boy
who was, from that moment, cured. He seems to be
suggesting that lunacy is caused by possession, thus
subverting the authenticity of his previously stated
categories. Fr Crehan has suggested that Christ was able
to discern which symptoms were of a natural cause and
which were, in fact, deliberately caused by the devil.[3]
The case of the bent woman, described by Luke, comes
into this category. Although outwardly she was suffering
from a sort of gouty contraction of the body, Christ
states, quite indisputably that she had been 'bound
by Satan these eighteen years'.

In the Acts of the Apostles we encounter examples
of possession where the possessed does not display
signs of physical illness as do the subjects described in
the gospels. There is, for example, the young slave-girl
Paul meets in Philippi. She was 'possessed with a spirit
of divination', and her masters made money from her
fortune-telling powers. The girl attaches herself to Paul,
dogging his footsteps and day after day shouting out:
'These men are the servants of the most high God,
which shew unto us the way of salvation'. Paul eventually
gets rather irritated and exorcizes the spirit: 'I command
thee in the name of Jesus Christ to come out of her!'
The demon leaves the girl, who is then useless for
exploitation by her owners.

Not exactly an exorcism in the formal manner, but
certainly a confrontation in which the forces of the
devil are associated with magic, is the case of Elymas

the sorcerer. This man deliberately attempts to prevent
Paul from spreading the Holy word and receives this
rebuke: 'O full of all subtlety and all mischief, thou
child of the devil, thou enemy of righteousness, wilt
thou not cease to pervert the right ways of the Lord?
And now behold, the hand of the Lord is upon thee,
and thou shalt be blind, not seeing the sun for a season.'
It is rare to find a possessed person being actually
punished in this way since it would suggest that the
individual is responsible for his acts and not, as in the
other cases, the visiting demon.

Christ, it seems, understood that only a few illnesses
were caused by demonic possession; furthermore, it also
appears that — no matter what later commentators have
said — Christ himself believed in demons. 'I beheld Satan
as lightning fall from heaven', he tells the seventy appointed to precede him on his travels. And their joy is expressed in the realization that 'even the devils are subject
to us through thy name'. This passage successfully dis-
proves the suggestion that Christ only pretended he was
dealing with devils in order to accommodate himself to
popular belief, for this is in intimate conversation with
his followers.

On another occasion, when the disciples have failed
to exorcize the lunatic boy, Christ tells them first that
their failure was due to their unbelief, but later adds,
almost as an aside 'this kind goeth not out but by
prayer and fasting'. This certainly has the casual, informative tone of an expert chatting with his apprentices.
Throughout, Christ speaks naturally and conversationally
about the devil and about demons and in circumstances,
such as those just cited, where there is no possibility that
he is either pretending or using general metaphors.

The New Testament exorcisms have certain characteristics, and lay down certain constants for both possession

and exorcism that are endemic to the Christian approach to the subject. The two dramatic exorcisms already described of the demoniac and the possessed Gadarene serve as basic examples.

First of all, the demon who possesses the subject, recognizes Christ immediately, and reacts defensively and with terror in the way in which, over subsequent centuries, demons have become traditionally expected to react to the artefacts or words associated with Christianity, and as vampires are supposed to quail before a crucifix.

This is an important feature: Christ presents himself and the demon reacts. Some commentators have attempted to build up circumstantial narratives around the Capernaum and Gadarene incidents in order to prove that the demoniacs already knew that Christ was around.[4] It is suggested that the man in the synagogue had heard other people referring to Christ as the Messiah, and that this prompted the demoniac fit. The gospels offer no such explanation and it seems unlikely anyway, since as already noted, Christ was not at this stage in his ministry regarded as the Messiah by anyone. Further, Christ commands the demon to be silent when he shouts of 'the Holy One of God'. This accords with other occasions when Christ silences demons because they know who he is. Such an attitude would suggest that, rather than the possessed person having heard of Christ's messiahship from others, he had prior information and that Christ was unwilling to risk the possibility of the general public learning of his function from a demon's mouth. In the fraught and possibly hysterical circumstances of such confrontations, the broadcasting of this information in such a way would seriously subvert Christ's mission, the nature of which would be revealed in good time. It might suggest, as indeed the Pharisees thought, that Christ was himself in league with the devil. In the Gadarene incident there is no evidence in any of the accounts that the demoniac could have heard about Jesus prior to their actual face-to-face meeting.

We must accept then, that the demons within the possessed men recognize Christ (by his very aura, perhaps, or just intuitively) and the subsequent dialogues of exorcism are conducted between Christ and the demon, the possessed person himself being unaware of what is happening. Christ's function, among other things, was to overthrow the kingdom of demons and, as stated by Matthew, to cast them into everlasting fire specifically prepared for 'the devil and his angels'. The lurking demons would recognize this agent sent to destroy them, which is a fundamental assumption of Christian exorcism.

This brings us to the second characteristic: Christ speaks directly to the demon. Those who reject the possibility of real demons being present in these cases and prefer to see the possessed as being deranged in the modern sense, argue that Christ was acting in something approaching the manner of the contemporary radical therapist. In essence this attitude suggests that social and cultural pressures force the individual to conform to certain fairly rigid patterns of behaviour. At any given time a percentage of people find themselves unable to conform. They may try, painfully perhaps, to adjust to society and live a somewhat distorted life-style. Or, if this is impossible they may begin to behave in a way that opposes the prevalent cultural standards and thus are categorized, by that culture, as mad. The traditional psychiatrist will see a cure in coming to terms with the condition and then adjusting it to cultural patterns. The radical therapist, however, will accept the patient's

own valuation of himself, will reject the idea of
personal therapy for a personal neurosis, and attempt
to initiate change rather than adjustment.

In a rudimentary way this does seem to be what
Christ was doing. Exorcism is a radical method of treatment and in accepting possession Christ is accepting the
patients' own valuations. Also the cures are based on a
tremendous change of attitude, rather than a simple
physical recovery. Exorcism prayers are always addressed
to the visiting demon.

A third characteristic of Christ's exorcisms, and perhaps connected with the radical therapy theory, is that
in all the examples referred to or narrated in detail by
the synoptists, no prayers or rituals are used. As we have
seen, rituals and use of objects, were characteristic of
exorcism at the time. But in Christ's case his word alone
is enough to cast out the devils. This must have been
largely due to his messianic charisma, but in any circumstances his vocal stamina must have been remarkable.
In Pier Paolo Pasolini's outstanding film of *The Gospel
According to Saint Matthew* (1968) which is extremely
faithful to the text, Christ comes across as a tireless,
impassioned speaker almost as if he himself were
possessed — as indeed he was, by the Holy Ghost.

The gospel narratives of exorcisms always state that
the demons, devils and unclean spirits depart from their
victims. But there are no accounts of their visual manifestation. In later centuries, accounts of exorcism frequently allow the demon to leave the possessed in some
palpable form: a mouse, a spider, a cloud of evil-smelling
smoke or some nameless horrible shape. Medieval
illustrations are particularly prone to visualizing demons
and perhaps at this time such proof was needed to
convince or support the beliefs of a credulous populace
and at the same time adding a touch of real terror to

the power of the Church.

No such circumstantial detail was required in Galilee (though as we have seen, the mass suicide of Gadarene swine could be read in this way). The convincing success of the exorcisms seems to have been ascertained by the behaviour of the patient after the alleged expulsion. The pattern of possession can be assumed as an extreme convulsion followed by a faint or coma, the victim then recovering and behaving normally. It is not recorded whether any of the demoniacs had a later relapse as has happened so often in the cases of 'miraculous' faith cures.

Physical recovery is documented fully enough: the blind see, the deaf hear, the lame are made straight. But the concept of exorcism was not evolved simply to perform rather difficult cures on the analogy of a physical operation or as a sort of divine aspirin. Christian exorcism has a double purpose; to remove the demon and then to fill the vacancy thus left with the Holy Ghost.

Christ says as much during his argument with the Pharisees: 'But if I cast out devils by the Spirit of God, then the kingdom of God is come into you'. This is most explicitly demonstrated in the case of the Gadarene who first prays that he may be allowed to accompany Christ, thus indicating that radical change in his attitude. Christ refuses him, but asks him to return to the city and to his friends and spread the word of God.

Whether one prefers to doubt the reality of the New Testament exorcisms and see them as parables of evil within society, or whether one accepts their documentary accuracy, the ultimate Christian message remains unchanged; exorcism in this context is not the triumph of ritual over superstition, but that of good over evil realized in the most positive way.

ALL THE OFFSPRING OF DEVILDOM

So the devil became real. He was visualized, described in minute detail, given characteristics, feared . . . and hunted. Hell became a reality too. It was dreamed about in horrible nightmares and described in mind-bending horror by haunted visionaries. 'The wretched bodies of the condemned shall simmer and blaze in these living fires . . . the fire is more deadly than any which man can suffer in his life . . . not to these torments will there be any measure of termination, there the sentient fire burns limbs and renews them, feeds on them and nourishes them.'[1] Such was the imagery, and the beliefs which the popes and preachers of the early church flung at their terrified flocks.

Today it is easy, perhaps too easy, to laugh at the simplicity and gullibility of the people who were thus terrorized and who built their lives around this fear. Tighter than any exorcist has ever managed to bind a demon, the Church bound its converts in iron bands of discipline, the slightest deviation from which, meant eternal damnation in the most appalling circumstances the mind of man could devise.

·Only two categories of people resisted this indoctrination: the witches and the scientists. The latter, while hardly resembling today's breed, did at least stand back a little, query everything and view all this with a little honest doubt. The witches, while paying lip-service to the new morality, quietly and with inevitable secrecy, returned to the old religions, the practices of their fathers and grandfathers with their creativity, sponteneity and fertile exuberance. But in any case, both categories were instant candidates for the stake.

The devil was hunted. But no matter how thoughtfully the theologians, the early saints and thinkers defined the devil, no matter how real they were able to make him in the imaginations of the people he was not, like a stag or a bear, visible to be chased and slaughtered. He could only be isolated when he chose to make his presence known through the behaviour of some unfortunate individual he had chosen to possess.

And so the great age of demonic possession, with its inevitable concomitants of exorcism, persecution, torture and even execution began. Distinctions were made, of course. A person deemed to be demoniacally possessed would be exorcized if possible — often by humiliating and painful means: exorcism was not always prayer, the accompanying *remedia corporalis* could involve the use of noxious fumes, vile potions, privations and distressing probings especially around the genital regions.

There were others who were judged, not to be possessed which was largely an involuntary condition, but to have made a pact with the devil and to be using the guidance of Satan for nefarious deeds. They were given a different sort of treatment. But sometimes the distinctions merged and many completely innocent but disturbed individuals were senselessly and cruelly persecuted.

It is not the function of this book to explore the meaning and activities of witchcraft. But since witches were often believed to be possessed by the devil as well as in league with him, the practice will be referred to frequently. By witchcraft I mean adherents of a religion that is older than Christianity and which was, for many centuries a viable alternative to it while not a deliberate nor therefore heretical opposition. Witchcraft itself is not assumed to have any connection with

Satanism which developed much later (along with Satan in fact) and which when mentioned will be clarified as such.

Manifestations of what we may call demonic possession began soon after the death of Christ, and by the fourth century had become a matter of concern. Until this time, it had been the general and benevolent attitude of the early Fathers to agree that even devils can achieve forgiveness — after, of course, a suitable period of binding and punishment. Such was the mercy of God.

By the fourth century, however, all that had changed. There was, as Eric Maple has expressed it 'a war in which there could be neither reconciliation nor compromise, a cosmic battle between the powers of creation and destruction for the most stupendous prize in the universe, the immortal soul of the whole human race.'[2]

This hardening of attitude meant that there could be no possibility of mercy at all for the devil whose demons would certainly abuse God's forgiveness. In exorcism then, as now, the devil was bound and sent to the place appointed him — presumably hell — until the day of judgement. There was not the slightest chance of redemption.

The exorcists and torturers themselves believed firmly that in practising their arts they were dealing with the revealed devil, revealed through the peculiar behaviour of the possessed. But it should be remembered that the unfortunate victims were in fact people, most often merely harmless, unhappy people: torture for deviation and punishment for madness begin here.

It has been recognized that in its need to establish itself the early Church wiped out most of what was valuable in paganism: critical thought, medical progress, the arts — those things that had reached a high stage of development in ancient Greece. The intellectual development of Europe was arrested for a thousand years. But possibly the most militant war waged by the Church was that against the pleasures of the flesh and its sensual delights.

The new moral code, inflexible and austere, must have presented some problems and confusions for people who had hitherto hardly thought about sex, inasmuch as it was regarded as a natural and unproblematic part of living. It has been argued that the comparatively modern concept of romantic love is the final rationalization of the Church's moral teaching which suggested that life-long monogamy was the only alternative to hell fire.

The strident erotophobia of St Paul has much to do with it. In his first letter to the Corinthians he puts his own attitude fair and square: he is unmarried, he says, and frankly wishes that all other men could be like that. But to those weaklings who were unable to forego sex completely, he offers the alternative of marriage which is better than burning. Canon Derrick Bailey, writing about sex in Christian thought comments that although during the first three centuries of Christianity there was little legislation regulating sexual relationships, 'from the earliest times we find precepts inculcating a high standard of moral conduct and threatening the delinquent with ecclesiastical or divine retribution'.[3]

But phallic worship was not easily eradicated and soon the Church had, perforce, to assimilate the impulse: Priapus became St Guignolet and his effigy became associated with the curing of sterility in women. In Rome, long after the official end of paganism, women wore phallic ornaments to church, much as they always had done when practising other, older forms of worship. The Church was, however, slowly managing to confine officially the natural sexual urges, and making all but the approved expressions of sex a form of heresy.

In 390 A.D. for example, Valentian instituted the practice of death by burning for homosexuals. In that precise context this recalls the punishment delivered in the legend to the inhabitants of Sodom. But of more general significance is the fact that burning was a previously unknown form of execution, and it certainly caught on as being the form of death penalty considered most appropriate for heretics of all kinds. Although many homosexuals were in fact burned at the stake over the succeeding centuries there seems to be no record of homosexuality *per se* being regarded as a form of demonic possession whereas some twentieth century exorcists do seem to view it as such.

Theodosius banned all other religions but Christianity in 395 A.D., thus ensuring that all pre-Christian forms took on the official stigmata of criminality. In 538 A.D. Justinian codified Roman Law, thus incorporating one religion's prejudice into the phrasing of the law — a fact that still exists on the statute books of America and England today with regard to so-called sexual offences. It is unlikely that adherents of the pre-Christian religions made spontaneous and eager conversions. All over Europe those whose previous forms of worship had included fresh air, music, dancing, food and drink and sexual rites must have found Christianity rather morbid.

It is quite likely that the pagan and other mystery cults of the time did contain elements of sacrifice and sexual activity that were dubious if not revolting. And maybe the lusty life of city and port included then — as it does so often today — exploitative and undesirable sexual elements. But to enforce a radical change of attitude whereby all sexual expression is clouded by fear and guilt, would produce much greater horrors.

For the long-term effects of this was to impose a black cloak of anxiety and guilt upon what were, in fact, the normal instincts of men and women. And when a situation arises in which frustration is combined with guilt then the results can be appalling.

By following Paul's conviction that the penalty of indulging in any form of sexual expression outside the structure of monogamous heterosexual marriage would most certainly bring the pain of hell's fires, the Church calmly and fatally handed over to the devil complete rule over the genitals, and consequently the entire function and principle of creation — human reproduction — came within his province.

This had a further significant result. By rejecting the creative principle in this fashion, the Church also inevitably rejected the very medium of creation — woman herself. Paul had forbidden women to raise their voices in church, but during this time all other sorts of liberties were slowly removed from women until they were reduced in status to the level of slaves useful only for breeding. In the sixth century a Church council held at Macon is recorded as having spent two whole days discussing whether a woman was, in fact, a human being or not. Only as nuns were women accorded any sort of recognition by the Church and clearly this was because by embracing this profession they had rejected any possible calls of the flesh. Such male chauvinism was to hold sway for centuries.

All kinds of distortions and cruelties resulted from these basic presumptions which were being so firmly interwoven with the very foundations of Christianity. Childbirth, for example, became a time of horror and disgrace, the visible and logical result of indulging in the sins of the flesh, with labour pains seen as an appropriate punishment. So why should attempts be made to relieve the agonies? Baptism was a form of exorcism by which the devil present in all new-born children (remnant of the original sin that created them) could be expelled — Hell had, at this time, a special section reserved for unbaptized infants. So if it came to making a decision between saving the life of a mother or her baby, then why bother with the mother who had sinned when the child could be saved for baptism and salvation?

The oppression of women and the repression of sexuality themselves are root causes of many symptoms of distress and neurosis with which today's psychiatrists must contend. And so it is not perhaps surprising to find that the most celebrated cases of so-called demonic possession happened among women in general and in convents in particular. Nor is it surprising that among the symptoms that came to be regarded as a sure sign of demonic possession were obscene language and sexually suggestive gestures.

Of course, there were to be a number of other causes of demonic attack, but the Church by outlawing the genitals certainly made them the most vulnerable chink in the armour of righteousness. Certainly their genitals were uppermost in the minds of the early saints, and some of the privations they inflicted upon themselves in order to defend their chastity and mortify their flesh described by Eric Maple in his lively book *The Domain of Devils* make amusing reading. However, the reality of the situations can scarcely have been funny.

St Jerome fled to the desert and sought escape by the honoured methods of fasting and prayer, only to relive the lusts of the cities in his luxurious dreams. Father Anthony repelled the devil several times, in his guise as a horde of fierce desert demons snapping like dogs, as a beautiful woman and finally as a black child who presented himself as 'the spirit of fornication'. The anchorite Pamphnutius was visited in his cell by a gorgeous lady demon, so he thrust his hands into the fire 'hoping by this act of homeopathic magic to suppress the fires in his groin'. Certainly the devil knew where these men's weakness lay. 'Simon Stylites stood upon one foot for a whole year ... St Mary of Egypt wandered for forty-seven years black with filth ... St Anthony never washed his feet, St Abram washed neither hands nor feet; St Sylvia only washed her fingers and St Hilarion never washed at all.'[4]

These were disciplines devised to ward off external temptations, temptations which existed perhaps only in the minds of these sad men and women who conjured voluptuous women and men from their dreams and turned the packs of dogs that ranged the deserts into hordes of demons. Had they at any time given way to the temptations of the flesh, they would certainly have regarded themselves as being possessed by a demon. St Godric managed to fend off the seduction techniques of a beautiful female demon who entered his cell, only to find himself being attacked by her with the furniture.

Medieval demons seemed much more prone to enter and take possession of a person than were the primitive ones who tended to tempt from a short distance. The idea of possession began to be taken very literally. It should be always remembered that virtually nothing was known about the human mind until the nineteenth century which meant a background of radical ignorance and great deal of both prejudice and superstition. And always in the background of consciousness were the New Testament stories of Christ expelling demons from the mad Gadarene and others.

So it was taken for granted that demons were actual physical things that entered a human body and left, under exorcism, from the natural orifices. Priests conducted exorcisms, but the ordinary people equipped themselves with many charms and devices for protection against the armies of demons. Iron, salt, and holy water were established repellants, so were certain prayers. Spilling salt laid one open to demonic attack, so one must fling some over the shoulder to blind the devil. Rude gestures, spitting and blowing on possible demonic sources were continually practised.

The celebrated story, attributed to Gregory the First, was told and re-told with embellishments. A careless nun ate a lettuce leaf without first crossing herself. As it happened a demon was sitting on the leaf and it was able to get into the unprotected woman. In one version the demon resists all attempts at exorcism on the grounds that it wasn't his fault if the nun forgot to take an elementary precaution.

Bishop Martin of Tours confronted a demonized man and, failing to exorcize him by loud commands and exhortations to the demon, forced his fingers into the fellow's throat and demanded that the devil eat them. A risky thing to do, since the man was violent. But sure enough the devil was too timid to chew on a Bishop so he made a humiliating exit by the rear, leaving 'sad and foul traces behind him'. St Bernard acquired considerable fame as an exorcist by expelling a devil that had entered a woman's mouth and St Norbert conducted an exorcism over a woman which resulted in the demon leaving her body with a cloud of sulphurous fumes.

Sometimes a note of unmagical realism crept in. St Bernard advised a woman who claimed that she was being raped nightly by a demon to lay about her with a big stick the next time it happened, which brought a swift end to that particular form of possession. St Francis was a noted exorcist. One of his followers, Brother Juniper was famous for taking asceticism too far and rejecting all forms of hygiene the result of which was that he could be smelt several yards away. When faced with a particularly intractable demon, St Francis would as a last resort threaten to call Brother Juniper whereupon the emissary of Satan would make himself scarce at once.

St Edward the Confessor himself performed a rather devious and agreeable form of exorcism. The story goes that the King, who had the power to see spirits, came across a devil dancing for joy on the latest pile of money brought in by the Danegeld tax which was being levied to pay for the war against the Danes. There is a pictorial representation of this particular demon in an illuminated text at Trinity College, Cambridge. It shows a rather friendly looking little figure with a hooked nose, pointed ears, horns, cloven feet and tail. The King realizing that Satan himself was delighted with the tax, immediately abolished it, thus confounding the devil and relieving the people of a very unpopular drain on their incomes.

Very few people contested the universally held beliefs about demons and possession, for even those whom we might think of as more enlightened individuals were still restricted by the limitations of the age. In 100 A.D. St Hildegard claimed that it was impossible for a demon to enter the human body. But her argument was disregarded because all around were people writhing in convulsions, screaming obscenities, twitching, groaning and displaying all the unmistakable signs of demonic possession. Sometimes they were thrown in the air and flung to the ground again; they spoke in strange tongues, could see into the future and were reduced to a state of abject terror by the presence of holy objects.

At the end of the fifteenth century two further complications were added to the general situation, and they were mainly the result of the publication of the *Malleus Maleficarum*, a manual for witch-hunters. The policy of the church had always been to suppress any stories about witches, particularly gatherings of witches and the idea that they were able to fly. In a document mentioned as early as 900 A.D., called 'The Canon Episcopi', it was stated that stories of witches' rides were but dreams and that good Christians should not believe such things. However, in 1484, Pope Innocent VIII produced his bull *Summis Desiderantes* in which he spoke of the immense harm being caused in the world by the devil and the supernatural. As a result two experienced witch-finders from the Tyrol and Basel, Domincans Heinrich Kramer and Jacob Sprengler set down their experience in the *Malleus* which ran into thirteen editions by 1520. It revealed a detailed picture of a Satanic witch cult and updated 'The Canon Episcopi' by suggesting that what was a dream on one occasion could be a true experience on another. The book became the most authoritative manual available.

The first result of this new influence was the promotion of the belief that one individual could induce possession in another, that is could bewitch him. So cases of possession were being less frequently attributed to the devil working alone and selecting individuals for visitation himself, and more to the action of other, malevolent, individuals in the community who were being used by the devil as his conscious agents. In this way the great witch hunts gathered momentum and the remedy for possession was not just exorcism of the possessed but also the discovery and punishment of the person, the witch who was responsible.

The second complication was one that must have caused both irritation and anxiety to many intelligent and rational individuals. It became almost impossible for anyone to be sceptical about possession or witchcraft in the sense of the witch as devil's agent with the power to bewitch. To express disbelief in witchcraft was virtually taken as an admission of being a witch. The physician Agrippa narrowly escaped thus being branded for his rational views.

In succeeding centuries some people were able to discount certain popular beliefs and to isolate obvious abuses, but they had to move carefully. The Dutch doctor Johannes Weyer was one of the first people to investigate clinically cases of diabolical possession and two Englishmen, Sir Reginald Scott and John Cotta took similar detached views. Joseph Glanvil who was a persecutor of witches produced in 1681 his *Saducimus Triumphatus* in which he admitted that it was 'very improbable that the devil, who is a wise and mighty spirit, would be at the beck of a poor hag, and have so little to do as to attend to the errands and impotent lusts of a silly old woman'.

This thought must have flitted across the minds of many who tortured and persecuted some poor old woman who happened to have a cat or was in some way deformed, as she was being pierced with needles in the search for an insensitive spot, or bound and flung into the village pond to see if she would float or sink. Yet for many even these thoughts were rationalized by the conviction that each individual witch was a part of the huge conspiracy of witches all deeply in league with Satan, and that every successful prosecution would be a blow to the whole organization. In this climate possession and its pendant, witchcraft, was encouraged to grow and flourish. Eric Maple writes: ' ... sixteen hundred years after the death of Christ vast areas of Europe presented the sorry spectacle of whole communities, utterly spell-bound, all vying with one another to produce the greatest number of gibbering demoniacs, screaming maniacs and foaming, leaping epileptics'.

Not unexpectedly, the most famous and detailed cases of mass demoniac possession tend to have happened in convents where they take on an unmistakable aura of sexual repression. Generally the claim is made by the nuns that they are being possessed — in both senses of the word — by male demons which were called incubi (the female demons who invaded the beds of monks were called succubi) which caused all the manifestations of their possession. One of the earliest cases on record happened to some nuns at Cambrai in France in 1491 shortly after the appearance of the *Malleus Maleficarum* when everyone was more than commonly alert for signs of possession. The nuns performed the characteristic actions of possession — barking like dogs, showing superhuman strength and having various kinds of fits. Finally, the nun who had first begun to have fits which communicated themselves to others, was discovered to be herself a witch. This situation would, as we shall see, repeat itself.

Johannes Weyer was a member of the investigating committee sent to inquire into an outbreak of demonic possession among the nuns of the convent of Nazareth at Cologne. Weyer, as already suggested, tended to deny the existence of witchcraft and sorcery. He did place great faith in exorcism, but preferred a rather sober form, involving prayer and fasting, to the more dramatic Roman rites. At the convent of Nazareth, Weyer noted the erotic origin of the manifestations the nuns were displaying. For example, their fits would consist of convulsive bodily movements; the nuns would lie on their backs, their bodies arched quite rigidly so that the pudenda are thrust forward in imitation of coitus — what is called the *arc-en-cercle* position. Afterwards Weyer noted that the nuns 'opened their eyes with apparent expressions of shame and pain'.

Weyer was heavily criticized as 'ignorant in matters of law, revolting in his theories and worthy of the most rigorous chastisement'. But however revolting, his theories had substance. In the case of the nuns of Nazareth it was discovered that the epidemic had started when a young girl who lived in the nunnery began fantasizing about having a man visit her. Nuns looking after her were unnerved by her convulsions and began to imitate them. But, as a matter of fact some lads from the neighbourhood had been climbing over the convent walls to enjoy the nuns. This had been stopped and it was then that the convulsions had started. Weyer discovered similar incidents in other nunneries and at an orphanage. Mass possession among children and young girls would also become a familiar event in these years.

Weyer (sometimes called de Weier) was being called 'the founder of modern psychiatry' and while subscribing to the established belief in devils managed to bring great scientific detachment to his investigations and his book *De Praestigiis Daemonum* is regarded as a classic work. He wrote:

> The uninformed and unskilled physicians relegate all the incurable diseases, or all the diseases the remedy for which they overlook, to witchcraft. In all such cases a good doctor is to be consulted because nothing is more important than to make the clinical situations as clear as daylight, for in no domain of human life are human passions so freely at play as in this one, these passions being superstition, rage, hate and malice.

The combination of an intense religiosity and sexual desire seems to have a peculiarly strong erotic charge. Nuns in lesbian or heterosexual couplings are a recurring theme in pornography, verbal and visual, down the ages to the present day. In a mild form, the motif is repeated in spates of down-market sexploitation films, often emanating from the Roman Catholic countries of Italy and France. There is, obviously, a high fantasy value here, and among modern artists, only Jean Genet seems to have explored it seriously.

When Weyer isolated the psycho-sexual neurosis that lay at the root of so much alleged demonic possession in convents, he was outraging his contemporaries with something that appears obvious to the most casual modern reader. As we have already noted, nuns occupied a special place in society being, to all intents and purposes, women who had rejected voluntarily the carnal pleasures of the world. The thought that these holy and virginal enclaves were actually scenes of vice must therefore have been particularly disgusting to their contemporaries, and such manifestations could only be the responsibility of the devil himself, or his agents.

The intense forms of punishment which the early Christian fathers inflicted on themselves were in reality an expression of sexual guilt fostered by the Church they served. A particularly extreme example is presented by Christine of Trond who, in the twelfth century lay in a hot oven, fastened herself to a wheel, had herself racked, hung on the gallows beside a corpse and then had herself partly buried in a grave.

The convents of the middle ages were not wholly filled by pure and innocent girls, however. Among the nuns were a number of women who were sexually experienced, either having been seduced or having had a sexual liaison which failed or caused them to be rejected by the families. Often becoming a nun was a kind of punishment. As at the convent of Nazareth at Cologne, local youths could always find access to willing nuns by climbing the convent walls.

The ceremony of consecration for a nun was planned to ressemble in many important respects, the ceremony of marriage. A ring was placed on her finger, and one of the responses she was required to make was : 'I love Christ into whose bed I have entered'. Moreover, the Church would receive any money the girls' parents had set aside for a dowry.

The atmosphere then was one of built-in conflict: the nuns were deprived of physical sex yet at the same time dedicated to the one perfect but unobtainable male. Mechtild of Magdeburg advised 'all virgins to follow the most charming of all, the eighteen-year old Jesus'. So there can be little wonder that erotic convulsions and phantom pregnancies were widespread. It is a familiar fact to the modern mind that those who enjoy a satisfactory sex life scarcely ever think about sex, yet those who are sexually deprived or frustrated elevate sex to the most important fact in their lives. Undoubtedly, priests abused the confessional by talking about sexual matters in great detail, ostensibly to warn the girls of the dangers of the flesh, but in reality working on their frustrated desires. But to the solid and respectable men and women living normal lives outside the convents, the manifestations within must have seemed doubly horrifying, and clearly caused by the malefic influence of diabolical possession.

Such outbreaks occurred with regular frequency, all over Europe in the sixteenth and seventeenth centuries. At Oldham on Rhine in 1577 a nunnery was supposed to have been invaded by sexually rampant dogs; in 1599 a group of nuns in Milan displayed symptoms of sexual hallucinations; in 1613 some nuns in Lille seemed to be leading a life of one long orgy and a similar outbreak in Madrid was quelled when the Inquisition with remarkable sense closed the convent and sent the nuns involved to other places.

In two of the most famous cases, an outside cause for the diabolical outbreaks was found — a scapegoat in the form of a magnetic male. The first, at Aix, occurred in 1609; the second was the notorious case of Loudon, an episode which seems to have a particular appeal for the twentieth century mind. Since Aldous Huxley's thorough analysis appeared in 1956, the subject has twice been filmed, turned into a play and an opera. Both cases followed a similar pattern: one or two nuns began to display signs of demonic possession which was communicated to the other inhabitants of the convent. The possessing demon made a public accusation, blaming an outside person for the disturbance; the person, a local priest, was arrested, tortured and executed, whereupon the possessions died down.

At the convent of Aix, the main hysteric was a young girl called Madeleine de Mandol. She developed manic depression, convulsed, made animal noises and screamed of sodomy and cannibalism. It was reported that when the demon made its presence known in her body it was possible to hear her bones grating against each other. Her bowels were displaced and turned upside down. Soon she was joined by another nun, also young, called Louise Capeau whose convulsions were equally violent. At one stage six men were able to stand on the rigid, arched body of Madeleine. Then, through the mouth of her demon, who was called Verrine, Madeleine accused the local priest, Louis Gaufridi, of being a magician and responsible for the demonic infestations.

Gaufridi was duly arrested and urged to confess. Since he was innocent he refused, and a full investigation was held. Apart from imprisonment and torture this included a search for the devil's mark. Such a search, part of the routine of witch-finding, was a particularly

nasty and humiliating experience. The theory was
that anyone who had made a pact with Satan would
have somewhere on his body a mark with which
the pact was signed. Moreover, this mark was understood to be insensitive to pain and incapable of
producing blood when pierced. It is not certain where
this idea originated; one possibility is that it had been
observed that stigmatization could occur among hy-
sterics (who would be regarded as possessed), and
that bleeding can be halted inexplicably by shock.
Expert witch-finders learned to distinguish between
the devil's mark and natural bodily blemishes —
moles, scars, birthmarks — but many people were
condemned on the strength of perfectly ordinary
pimples and warts.

The suspect, stripped and shaved of all hair which
might conceal some magic amulet, was then punc-
tured, virtually all over, with a bodkin until the
unfortunate person was a mass of blood. Since the
devil held sway over the genitals this was the area
where the closest examination was made, with special
attention to the anus of a male and the vagina of
a female.

A vindictive, or over-enthusiastic witch-hunter often
cheated. He might give the victim a sharp stab with
the needle, and while the wound was still smarting,
quickly reverse the instrument giving a gentle touch
with the blunt end which of course would pass
unnoticed by the victim. Bodkins with hollow shafts
and retractable needles (rather like stage daggers)
were actually manufactured. There were responsible
witch-finders who deplored and exposed these practices. In the case of Louis Gaufridi, three devil marks
were found on his body.

Eventually Gaufridi thought it best to confess, but

later retracted his confession and was sentenced to death in the usual manner reserved for heretics — slow burning. But he was first tortured in order to find out the names of his accomplices — witches were always regarded as part of a great conspiracy. His limbs were dislocated and he was racked. By some act of clemency he was strangled before being burned. After his death the devils left Madeleine de Mandol who resumed her interrupted life of piety.

The story of the devils of Loudon has been thoroughly expounded, but it is still debated whether the central figure was genuinely possessed or whether she was an absolute fraud or an hysteric. She was Sister Jeanne des Anges who at the comparatively early age of twenty-five was made Mother Superior of a small Ursuline convent at Loudon in Vienne. She was slightly deformed, having one shoulder higher than the other and in her youth had compensated for the boredom of convent life by cultivating an impressive saintliness which included ecstatic visions. In later years she wrote an autobiography which reveals a quite remarkable sense of self-awareness.

An attractive man called Urbain Grandier was the focus of Sister Jeanne's hysteria. He was the parish priest of St Pierre de Marche in Loudon; he was cultivated and worldly but lacking in discretion. He was twenty-seven when he arrived in Loudon and thirteen years later was arrested on a charge of immorality as his scandalous relationships with several young girls in the town were public knowledge. He, however, was able to duck the charge.

Sister Jeanne, wanting to get to know him better, invited him to become confessor to the convent, but Grandier refused. As it turned out this was an even greater mistake than allowing his sex-life to become public, for Sister Jeanne interpreted this rejection personally.

There was a further element in the situation. Grandier had acquired enemies among his colleagues in the Church and it seems that a certain conspiracy to discredit him developed. The local ringleaders (including the Public Prosecutor Trincant by whose daughter Grandier had an illegitimate child) turned to Father Mignon who was the confessor to the nuns. It appears that under this man's influence the nuns began to show signs of demonic possession, led by Sister Jeanne herself. There were convulsions, erotic postures, public masturbation, changes of voice and claims of being tormented by demons.

At the height of one such attack a nun mentioned the name of Grandier and was rapidly supported by the others. Sister Jeanne confirmed this and went further by naming the seven demons which Grandier had sent into her. Father Mignon also secured Grandier's name from the nuns under exorcism. Archbishop Sourdis of Bordeaux alarmed at the growing scandal, stepped in and declared that the nuns were not possessed and that the exorcisms were to stop and that no one else was to try and exorcize them. This immediately put a stop to the nuns' convulsions.

Matters might have rested there and the incident forgotten. But Grandier had now acquired an even more powerful enemy in Cardinal Richlieu who had a strong motive of his own for perpetuating the case. Richlieu wanted to revive the Inquisition and hoped to revoke the Edict of Nantes which allowed freedom of worship to all denominations. Great public exorcisms would be ideal to impress the Protestants.

So Grandier was arrested and convicted and three exorcists dispatched to Loudon. They were a Capuchin, a Franciscan and a Jesuit, Father Surin. Under their suggestive ministrations which were witnessed by crowds of susceptible people, the symptoms of possession returned with even greater violence to the nuns. Sister Jeanne now added the detail that Grandier had bewitched the sisters by throwing a bouquet or roses over the convent wall.

Grandier suffered the same treatment as Gaufridi had before him; his buttocks and testicles were deeply pierced with needles in a search for the devil's mark, and four insensitive places were found on his body. Proof of his guilt was guaranteed by the production in court of an alleged pact he had made with the devil and signed by Satan, Lucifer, Beelzebub, Leviathan and Astaroth. This document was written backwards, in mirror writing, following the widely held belief that the devil did things backwards. The prosecution produced this pact in all seriousness, even adding that the demon Asmodeus (who Sister Jeanne had identified as one of her invaders) had removed it from the devil's filing cabinet. This piece of nonsense was taken seriously and Grandier was found guilty. The tortures to which he was subjected were extreme — a contemporary writer records that the marrow oozed from his broken bones — and though assured that he would be strangled before being burned, the Capuchin friars had knotted the rope in such a way that it could not be drawn tight enough. So Urbain Grandier was burned alive.

The possessions did not stop however. Moreover the incident had reached the proportions of a national scandal. So, to justify the execution of Grandier, Sister Jeanne had to be exorcised once again. The Jesuit Surin was appointed to be her spiritual adviser. But this time, apparently, the exorcisms were not the dramatically-laden public ones, but much more carefully considered. Father Surin wrote in his autobiography: 'I was even more determined than ever to follow the path of penitence and prayer in making these nuns serve God with more fervour than before'. He himself offered 'to be burdened with Jeanne des Anges' evil and to feel all the sensations so far as being possessed by the devil, provided it pleases his divine goodness'. Here we have an example of the exorcist and the possessed changing roles, though Surin clearly did not feel that the dangers of demonic transference were as dangerous as some other exorcists, particularly modern ones, seem to believe.

His work with Sister Jeanne and the other nuns was partially successful but Surin was recalled before all the demons had left the Mother Superior and one called Zabulon said he would never leave her except at the tomb of St Francis de Sales. So she visited the tomb in Italy and was finally freed.

Sister Jeanne entered, then, an even more sensational phase of her eventful life, a phase which involved visions, prophecies and miraculous healings and was even said to have developed stigmata — the names of Jesus, Mary, Joseph and Francis de Sales — on her left hand.

There is no doubt today that Grandier was innocent of all the charges laid against him, though he was inevitably psychologically guilty. The sexual character of Jeanne's hysteria is completely obvious. She herself, in her writings, was particularly open about it. Seven demons had possessed her, she claimed. The first was Asmodeus who had filled her head with sexual fantasies, and the fourth was called Isaacaron who had aroused her passion by more direct methods. Plain and unloved, feeling herself rejected by the local sexual idol, her tensions combined with masturbation fantasies created the hysterical outbursts.

In a world that knew nothing of the complex workings of the mind and to which open description of sexual acts amounted to obscenity and blasphemy, the devil would clearly be seen at work. Sister Jeanne is remarkable in that she had the insight and honesty to see and to recount the inner process of her oppression. That she attributed it to demons and the work of Grandier should not be put down as vindictive malice, but to the narrow limits of knowledge and the profound nature of her belief.

The last notable case of possession in a convent to follow the same pattern as those of Aix and Loudon took place in the middle of the eighteenth century. Sister Maria Renata was the sub-prioress of the Premonstratensian convent of Unterzell near Wurzburg in Germany. She had entered the convent when she was nineteen, and at the time of her death in 1749 at the age of seventy — she had been sub-prioress for five years, so had lived a life of untroubled devotion for many years. In 1745 a young girl called Cecilia Pistorini entered the convent as a novice. Sister Renata was opposed to the girl, feeling she was unsuitable for convent life. She considered that the young woman was hysterical and prone to delusions. Sister Cecilia suffered from cramps and contortions, writhed on the ground, foamed at the mouth and cried out during periods of worship. She displayed all the signs of being possessed. Some of the other nuns began to suffer from the same afflictions. Because she was sceptical and not very sympathetic, Sister Renata became unpopular in the convent and the climax came when an older nun on her deathbed, accused Sister Renata of having bewitched her. As always accusation was tantamount to conviction and the elderly woman was duly arrested, tried and tortured. Exorcisms and penitential exercises were conducted, but the nuns remained possessed. Only the death of

Sister Renata would free them. She was allowed to be beheaded before being burned.

Priests, chaplains and spiritual directors seemed to have been the targets for attack by the possessed nuns in all cases. At Louviers in 1644 the nuns accused two priests one of them already dead, of bewitching them. They were duly burned, the dead one being exhumed. And in 1731 Catherine Cadière of Toulon accused her confessor Giraud of seduction.

Virtually all the documented cases of convent possession point to psycho-sexual hysteria. The unhappy story of Sister Renata may be an exception though even there the possibility of sexual tension of a lesbian nature cannot be completely discounted. That the outbreaks always seem to have started with one individual but quickly communicated themselves to others around them, suggests that a desire to attract attention was an important function of so-called possession.

This kind of mass-possession never seems to have been so fashionable in Protestant countries. This was probably because the Protestant faiths tended to be rather more austere and also, to be wary about believing in demons and spirits. In cases of apparent possession the sombre techniques of prayer and spiritual sustenance were pursued rather than the elaborate and dramatic ceremonies of Roman exorcism, which would be less satisfactory for the demanding hysteric. In England, particularly, there are very few cases of possession among adults, but English adolescents seem to have been as sensitive as French nuns, and there are many cases involving children.

One of the earliest recorded cases of mass possession among children, however, happened in Amsterdam in 1566 when some thirty youngsters began to display the symptoms — convulsions, foaming at the mouth, falling

about. Exorcism by the solemn Protestant methods
failed and the unhappy parents decided to risk heresy
and consulted magicians who were equally unsuccessful.
In fact the situation got worse as the children started to
vomit pins and needles and other small objects. Witchcraft was suspected and suitable victims found.

Vomiting small domestic objects and unsavoury items
seems to be a characteristic of child possession. In
Louvain in 1571 a fifteen year old girl started vomiting
hair, filthy water, substance resembling the dung of doves
and geese and shavings of wood. Exorcism by a priest
apparently cured her, but a contemporary writer admits
there may have been some deception.

In another case that occurred in Vienna in 1583, a sixteen year old girl complained of cramps and a group of
Jesuits spent eight weeks exorcizing her. Eventually they
claimed to have expelled no less than 12,652 living
demons from her which her grandmother had been keeping as flies in a jar. The poor grandmother was then
tortured into a confession of witchcraft and burnt to
death.[5] Social attitudes to children in the sixteenth and
seventeenth centuries were not those of today; children were incorporated into the adult world much
earlier, and the separate stages of childhood and adoles-
cence were virtually unmarked — children were, for
example, put into small versions of adult clothes almost
as soon as they could walk. Nevertheless, they did
retain that aura of purity and uncontaminated innocence.
The accusation from a child would therefore carry much
the same sensational import as that from a nun. Parents,
priests and other authorities took what children had
to say quite seriously. The most famous case of child
possession in England happened in 1589 when the ten-
year-old daughter of Robert Throckmorton, squire of
Warboys in Huntingdon began to have fits. She blamed

these on a respectable elderly neighbour, and soon her
four sisters were also having fits. Though the parents
were sceptical of the alleged cause they did confront
the old woman with the girls whose fits became worse.
The situation continued for over a year, becoming a
local scandal. At last, the elderly neighbour ceremonially
ordered the children to stop, which they did, thus
proving her a witch. She, and her daughter, were found
guilty and executed.

Other, similar cases, happened during the next few
decades. An interesting example, which gives an insight
into the general state of beliefs in England regarding
magic, witchcraft, possession and exorcism, occurred
in 1596 at Burton-on-Trent in Nottinghamshire. A
fourteen-year-old boy, Thomas Darling became sick,
had fits and claimed he could see green angels and
green cats. The doctor was unable to cure him and
when it emerged that the boy's convulsions became
much worse when the first chapter of St John's gospel
was read aloud, the conclusion was that he had been
bewitched. A local woman, regarded as a witch, was
accused and when Thomas confronted her he immediately
fell into an impressive session of thirty-seven consecutive
fits. The woman, Alse Gooderidge was condemned to
death but died first in prison.

However, Thomas Darling's fits continued and the
family sought the services of John Darrell. This interesting individual was born in Mansfield in Nottinghamshire and studied law at Cambridge before being
ordained. In 1586 he exorcized a girl in his native
town who had accused another woman of bewitching
her. Darrell supported this charge, but it was dismissed
by the magistrate who severely reprimanded Darrell
for his part in the business, threatening him with
punishment if he did anything similar again.

He ignored the warning and after he had successfully exorcized Thomas Darling by praying over the boy, he was called in on another case involving children. Here the two young children of Nicholas Starkie were suffering from the torments of possessing demons. A wandering conjuror had been called in and his charms and herbs had worked for a while, but after arguments with Starkie over money, the childrens' fits began again and spread to other children and the servants. There was a non-stop outbreak of fits, vomiting blood, shouting and barking. Eventually the conjuror was charged with witchcraft and hanged. But the fits did not end, the seven children and servants now involved continued their frightful antics and Darrell was called in. At once he began his exorcism which took three days of prayers and fasting before the demons fled. This was Darrell's most spectacular success but soon afterwards he was involved in an exorcism that brought about his downfall. This one also involved an adolescent boy who in the course of being exorcized accused several women of bewitching him. But the magistrates were suspicious and under pressure the boy admitted that his possession was a fraud and also that Darrell had instructed him in the details.

Darrell was examined by the Bishop of London and among the witnesses were Thomas Darling and the other adolescent, both of whom testified that their experiences of possession and the subsequent exorcisms by Darrell were faked and that Darrell had taught them to imitate the behaviour of the first girl he had exorcized in Mansfield several years before. Darrell and his colleague, a minister, George More, were imprisoned, their careers as exorcists at an end. Darrell protested his probity throughout the trial.

It was after the case of Darrell that the seventy-second

Canon of the Canons of London drawn up by Bishop
Bancroft in 1604 was framed. It forbids any Church
of England minister to 'attempt upon any pretence
whatever either of possession or obsession by fasting
or prayer, to cast out any devil or devils, under pain
of imposture or cozenage, and deposition from the
ministry'. Since that time no clergymen of the Church
of England have been allowed to practise exorcism
without a licence from their Bishop.

Examples of possession among youngsters can be
multiplied, but most seem to have been blatant frauds.
One boy created a sensation in 1620 by passing blue
urine and claiming to be bewitched. He was later
discovered to be putting ink into his chamber pot and
pushing ink-soaked paper under his foreskin. A desire
to be the centre of attention — a need obviously also
felt by some exorcists like Darrell — may have been a
contributory factor and also spite against some elder person who had upset or even frightened the child. In country
communities it was easy to cast blame on a particular
person who already had a reputation for being a witch.
But mixed in with these imaginative performances were
genuine cases of epilepsy, delusions and mental unbalance. To separate them was impossible when medicine,
magic and the Church were so closely interlinked and
when madness was regarded as being Satanically inspired.
And while the devil held sway as an absolute reality in the
minds of the populace, fear and superstition flourished.

Only when witchcraft and demonic intervention are a
naturally accepted part of the texture of everyday life
can such outbreaks happen. It was this sort of background of belief that allowed the much more serious
case of the witches of Salem in New England to
happen and work its way through to a horrible conclusion in which twenty-two people were finally executed

on the strength of the malevolent fantasies of a group of adolescent girls.

But the times were changing rapidly; while the New England township was being shattered with superstition and terror, in Europe the idea of witchcraft was being officially relinquished. In 1736 the penal laws against witchcraft were crossed off the statute books in England. The last death sentence passed on a witch was in 1712 on Jane Wenham, known as the 'wise woman of Walkern' in Hertfordshire. Her accuser was the servant girl of a local minister who claimed to have fits, and to see cat-devils with Jane Wenham's face, which urged her to kill herself. She also performed the now familiar domestic demonic trick of vomiting pins and needles. The wise woman was convicted, but later pardoned.

A doctor examined the servant girl and told her to wash her hands and face twice a day. He also advised that she should be kept under observation, recommending a 'lusty young fellow' for the job. Sure enough, the fits ceased and the girl later married her keeper. Only a few years earlier the witch would have been hanged and the girl made to suffer the fasting, prayers, and the exhortations to sanctity of the exorcists. The age of reason was dawning.

When we read that in the sixteenth century exorcism prayers were accompanied by such ministrations as bleeding the patient and forcing odd herbal mixtures down her throat, it can be seen that some glimmering awareness of physical cause was present. The link between physical symptoms and mental oppression had yet to be made, also the realization that many symptoms were of physical origin only. As the eighteenth century progressed these elements were to be isolated and examined. T. K. Oesterreich whose study of possession remains a classic, comments: 'Possession begins to disappear among civilized races as soon as belief in spirits loses power'. The devil was in retreat; beliefs in his witch-agents were dying and the exorcist relinquished his function first to the doctor, then much later, to the psychiatrist. Satan kept quiet. But he was merely biding his time, seeking new ways to make his presence felt.

4

AGES OF REASON

In the eighteenth century, the English social satirist William Hogarth produced an engraving which he called *Credulity, Superstition and Prejudice.* It shows the interior of a crowded church, dominated by a preacher, his wig askew, preaching hell-fire from a high pulpit. Two puppets dangle from his fingers; one a witch on a broomstick complete with cat, the other a typical devil with wings, tail, and grid-iron. In a corner are copies of the sermons of John Wesley and a translation of the *Malleus Maleficarum,* on them a barometer marked in degrees of possession, ranging from suicide up through madness, despair, settled grief and agony to lust, ecstasy, convulsive fits and once again, madness: a psychiatric graduation that would not be dismissed by today's practitioners.

Through the window a mysteriously oriental person gazes on the congregation all of whom are in the grip of some kind of superstitious agony. A woman lies in child birth and a stream of little rabbits are racing from beneath her skirts — it was commonly believed that a bewitched woman would give birth to unnatural progeny, usually leverets or kittens. A tiny demon stands on tip-toe to whisper into a man's ear and beside a copy of the *Demonologie* written in 1597 by James I (who felt that the best use of tabacco smoke was to exorcize demons) a man vomits strange objects.

As in Hogarth's other works — such as *The Rake's Progress* and *Marriage à la Mode* — he brings to his observations, a corrosive wit and cynical detachment, but also a feeling of pity for the credulous. In one

engraving he summed up the climate in which a belief
in witchcraft and a reliance on trivial superstition could
flourish and without doubt a similar composition could
be created today, drawing on the symptoms of the
strongly renewed interest in the occult.

The works of Hogarth and others provide a salutory
antidote to the vague image of the eighteenth century
as an age of reason. Legislation does not always produce
an instant change in public attitudes, as campaigners
realize. So although the witch laws were repealed, a
belief in witchcraft and the supernatural persisted quite
powerfully at grass-root level. And while the exclusive
domain of the priest and magician was being invaded by
demands for a more scientific approach, most cases of
mental illness were still firmly attributed to demonic
possession both by the sort of people Hogarth was
drawing, and indeed by many thinkers, particularly
among the clergy.

Examples of possession become less frequent as the
eighteenth century progressed. In Bristol in 1788 a
demoniac suddenly appeared in the streets announcing he
was possessed by the devil and proving it in the time-
honoured way by barking and screaming at passers-by,
and jumping and writing unpleasantly on the ground.
Seven priests were summoned and they worked for several
hours on the exorcism rituals until no fewer than seven
devils were seen to leave the exhausted fellow.

John Wesley, himself no stranger to psychic experiences, took what one might call the British public-school
attitude to the insane. He believed that Satan was responsible for disease, but his recipe for madmen was
that they should be put under a waterfall, or made to
eat nothing but apples for a month, on the principle
that cleanliness was next to godliness and that a healthy
body created a healthy mind.

Although the ruthless stranglehold that the Church had on both the minds and bodies of men was slowly loosening it would be another century before the bonds were really torn away. Nevertheless, the gloomy mixture of prayer and cruel physical privations was already falling into disuse. The writer John Bunyan describes an exorcism a century earlier in which a man, apparently suffering from a tumour of some sort, was bound face downwards on a bench, his face thrust into a bowl of smoking coals. This failed to expel the devil, and the fellow died. But in the eighteenth century the foundations of modern medicine and surgery were being laid.

Towards the end of the century attitudes to mental illness were beginning to change and the radical new idea that madness was a disease began to be voiced. Ultimately this would lead to the dangerous analogy of mind and body, but it was at least an improvement on the belief that madness was the result of demonic intervention.

Perhaps the first person to regard insanity as a disease was a seventeenth century English physician Thomas Willis, who was primarily a chemist. Later, in the eighteenth century, a German Roman Catholic priest, Joseph Gassner, began to explore what we would call psychotherapy. Ironically he did this through exorcism, believing that the majority of diseases were the result of demonic possession. But instead of regarding exorcism as a form of religious magic, Gassner saw it was the appropriate method of approaching his parishioners' fixed ideas about themselves.

The most serious research, however, was done in France. If exorcism had failed, as it invariably would in cases of severe mental unbalance, then the only answer for the demoniacs, as they were assumed to be, was to throw them into lunatic asylums. Jean Esquirol, one of the pioneers of reform, described how the typical

European asylum contained naked, ill-fed wretches who slept on straw in filthy, unventilated, and unlit cells. The more violent patients were frequently chained and in England, lunatics were often exhibited like animals in a side-show for the amusement of the public.

But as Robert Thomson has pointed out in his history of psychology, the reformists were doing something rather more than spearheading a humanitarian attack on cruelty and squalor. One of the leading reformers, Philippe Pinel was one of the first great psychiatrists. When put in charge of the Bicetre asylum in 1793 he removed all fetters and chains, gave the patients good food and occupations and as much freedom as possible. In his *Rake's Progress* series, William Hogarth illustrated Bedlam with half-naked, chained inmates with fashionable women holding up their fans in affected horror at the spectacle they have volunteered to witness. A roughly contemporaneous painting from France, however, shows the chains being removed from the inmates of an asylum there after the intervention of Pinel. That the main figures happen to be attractive young women in various stages of disarray does not detract from the argument.

The work of Pinel and Esquirol had an undertone of support from the Church. In 1780 the Abbé Betholin was writing: 'Demonology does not exist. It is a remarkable fraud or must be classed with other illnesses that are analogous to it'. In England too there were also signs of a new way of looking at these problems. There was a lunatic asylum in York where a Quaker woman died in mysterious circumstances. Among her fellow Quakers there was William Tuke who pioneered in York a hospital for the treatment of those who would previously have been thrown into asylums. The Society of Friends built the hospital which became a model for mental homes, its working based on the same sort of principles as those which were beginning to apply in France.

All this finally routed the old beliefs in demonology. Pinel employed a statistical approach to his clinical data and isolated psychological stress as a cause of mental illness and categorized the precipitating factors: financial anxieties, disappointment in love, bereavement. He was also the first person to use the term hallucination as the product of brain disturbance in which the patient sees or hears what is not there.

Equally important, progress was also being made in different but relevant fields: in the area that today we call parapsychology — the study of means of communication by other methods than through the senses and which is conveniently labelled by the Greek letter psi. In religion psi has always been of vital importance as we find when certain divine gifts are translated into parapsychological terms. Thus precognition is prophecy; clairvoyance is revelation; telepathy emerges in prayer and psychokinesis is the answer to prayer by physical miracles. It is this field of enquiry that explains why so many characteristics that were once regarded as indubitable signs of demonic possession can be justified by natural means: the appearance of stigmata on a body, supernormal strength, foretelling the future among them.

Parapsychology is a modern science, of course, but the change of thinking which allowed men seriously to reject the concept of divine agency as the sole cause of so many puzzling manifestations was happening in the eighteenth century. The idea of a natural principle was attractive, but it could not be formulated until men were at the cultural stage when they could grasp general laws that might explain natural phenomena. And at this period the science of physics was emerging which paved the way, precisely, for such an acceptance.

A powerful contribution was made by Franz Mesmer who has been called the father of modern hypnotism. Although his work caused an initial sensation Mesmer and mesmerism aroused the fury of scientists and he fell out of favour and actually died in obscurity. Mesmer used magnets, mysterious passes, a giant battery and incidental hypnotism to work his cures, which gave him a certain fashionable cachet in Paris. He soon discovered that the magnets were irrelevant and ascribed his cures to animal magnetism which existed universally in the human body and flowed from the finger tips. Although quickly devalued, Mesmer's ideas did encourage rational thought on the subject and the foundations were laid for exploring the possibilities of communication with the spirit world.

Everywhere the bastions of faith and superstition were being eroded; Voltaire wrote ceaselessly and dynamically, his books were continually burned by the outraged clergy. Fifty of them were placed on the Papal index and he himself so hounded that he was writing under more than 130 pseudonyms. Tom Paine attacked the foundations of Christianity, but the Church fought back, if from an increasingly entrenched position.

There were always preachers only too willing to reassert the existence of Satan and to breathe hell fires from their pulpits. The law was always on the Church's side when it came to teaching its critics a lesson by the prison or the pillory. This continued through the nineteenth century and, in fact, it was not until 1967 that, with the abolition of censorship in the theatre, blasphemy became possible in the theatre. As late as 1886, Dr Pankhurst, father of the famous suffragette, was involved in a court case because of a blasphemous statement he made.

A final example of the conflict that was engaged between science and established dogma is found in what one might reasonably suppose to be the least dangerous and controversial fields of exploration, geology. Opposition to geology on religious grounds remained particularly strong up until the beginning of the nineteenth century. The discovery that the age of the earth extended backwards by millions of years flung a very contentious gauntlet before the Bible itself.

The truth of God was under attack and charges of demonic perversion were quickly levelled at geologists by an acutely distressed Church. Geology was dubbed 'this dark art', but quite quickly it was discovered that the six days of creation described in the Bible actually meant six massive periods of time. It was said that the eminent geologist Hugh Miller committed suicide in 1856 because his own findings were in direct contradiction to his own religious beliefs.

In 1859 Darwin published *The Origin of the Species,* and sacred science took its final body blow. It didn't die without a struggle, but the Church had eventually to reconsider its position on these fundamental issues. By the end of the nineteenth century the scientific worlds of geology, medicine, physics, anthropology, and psychology, had managed to eradicate almost all irrational beliefs based on religious teachings. Among these beliefs were ideas about demonologies, demonic possession and the devil. As these once vital factors could now be explained to everyone's satisfaction on scientific grounds, the ancient rite of exorcism naturally enough fell into abeyance, along with all other remnants of medieval superstition. The task of healing disturbed minds was taken from the Church and placed in the hands of psychiatry.

The devil had been exorcized once and for all, not by

prayer and fasting in the end, but by logical thought
backed by discovery of much more about the workings
of the mind. The twentieth century might reasonably
be expected to be completely demon-free, its children
rid of witchcraft and possession. And for a while this
seemed to be the case. Thus the revival of interest in
exorcism in the early 1960s caused a little consterna-
tion. Satanic cults were emerging all over Europe,
people gathering together to conduct rites which, they
hoped, would raise the devil. In 1963 there was an
incident in Germany in which a group of people terrorized a man believing they were conducting an exorcism.
Meanwhile similar things were happening in England. The
occult explosion was underway. It is axiomatic that an
interest in occult matters will embrace an interest in exorcism which in its attempt to communicate with a demon,
is part and parcel of the whole range of psychic experience
many individuals in Europe and America were seeking.

Occult means unseen, hidden, things beyond the range
of ordinary knowledge, and the term embraces an extremely wide range of activities. A guidebook to 'occult,
mystical, religious and magical London' includes information about esoteric, occult and magical groups, astro-
logers, palmists, hypnotists, psychotherapists, psychical
associations, clairvoyants, mediums, psychometrists, psychic healers, tarot and card dealers. It's an odd mix
with the largely respectable profession of psychotherapy
stuck among the fortune-telling and ectoplasm. Other
items may be added, including Satanic cults, witchcraft
black and witchcraft white, ouija boards and the *I Ching,*
even glancing at your instant horoscope in the morning
paper. And, of course, the recently established alternative churches such as Anton Szandor La Vey's Church
of Satan in America and the Process Church of the
Final Judgement, founded in London but now in

America, in addition to such variants as the dubious but strongly supported scientology movement.

As we have noted, officially sixty per cent of Americans believe in the devil; it is estimated that ten thousand people are engaged in witchcraft in Germany and the estimate for Britain is three times as many with covens in every university. It has been reported that in the Birmingham area alone there are no less than twenty-four known covens. Evidence of black magic groups emerges from time to time, usually through court cases involving vandalism in churchyards or, as had happened in America, through evidence of ritual slayings and suicides, the discovery of mass burials. An extra feature of the scene in Britain has been that the techniques of voodoo cults have appeared, something attributed to the increase of the immigrant population from the West Indies during the past decade.

Altogether this suggests a growing, if somewhat dispersed mass movement away from the Christian Church, and indeed away from all other forms of orthodox religion as well. There has also been a matching rise of interest in alternative forms of Christian witness.

> Everywhere, the observer of the American scene finds symptoms of what one has called religious revival . . . he finds them in the churches with their rapidly increasing membership, he finds them in the mushroomlike growth of sects. He finds them on college campuses and in the theological faculties of universities. Most conspicuously he finds them in the tremendous success of men like Billy Graham and Norman Vincent Peale, who attract masses of people Sunday after Sunday, meeting after meeting.[1]

So wrote Paul Tillich of Harvard's Divinity School in 1960. Since then the symptoms he noticed have certainly increased with the growth additionally of the pentecostal and charismatic churches of the early 1970s and the emergence of the Jesus movement in America and England. One might also point to the now settled adherents of oriental mysticism such as transcendental meditation, yoga, tai chi and the well-organized Hare Krishna sect.

One thing which all these symptoms do not suggest is that cool, clear-headed, scientifically-detached approach to life which might have been expected to develop during the twentieth century. What they seem to suggest, in fact, is a definite and positive search for some guidance and support from outside the world of technology, materialism and increasingly depersonalized society. And in this context the encounter group movement so strong in the U.S.A. and growing in the U.K. is also part of the whole picture. So is the dependance of younger people on certain categories of hallucinogenic drugs, and not entirely irrelevant are the slavish cults built up around minor pop stars.

Taking all these different and sometimes opposing examples as aspects of the same undefined urge, Paul Tillich again offers an insight when he writes of religion as 'the state of being concerned about one's own being and being universally'. He suggests that there are 'many people who are ultimately concerned in this way who feel far removed from every historical religion. It often happens that such people take the question of the meaning of their life seriously and reject any historical religion for just this reason. They feel that the concrete religions fail to express their profound concern adequately.'

Tillich was speaking only about religious revivals, but the sense in which he defines being religious can certainly apply to the motives of many who attach themselves to various occult groups. Considerable anxiety has been expressed, mainly by the conservative press and Christian spokesmen, about the spread of the occult interest.

There are three main ways of regarding this pheno-menon. The first may be described as materialist; that it is all nonsense. Playing with ouija boards or attending magical rituals might be fun for those whose taste lies in that direction, but they have absolutely no validity.

The second attitude is that there is a great deal of value in the search for the genuine occult and psychic experience, but that the subject must be approached with care and some discrimination. This attitude would embrace religious (in the orthodox sense) practices too.

The third attitude is specifically Christian, and rejects the entire occult scene as entirely pagan and therefore master-minded by the devil. The Christian looks to the fate of Elymas the sorcerer, and to the clairvoyant slave-girl that Paul exorcized, even though she was speaking the truth. Soothsaying and sorcery were part of the mystery cults and their associated life-style that existed with early Christianity and which were severely put down by the Fathers of the Church.

But whatever the viewpoint, from sceptical to frankly terrified, most people who have studied, or have been practically involved with, occultism agree upon one thing: that the occult is a potentially bad influence on the neurotic, the weak-minded and the insecure.

Obviously not everyone who plays with an ouija board, or even becomes a practising member of a coven, ends up in a mental hospital. But certainly the casualties of the occult are those who hit the headlines decapitated or jailed for perverse activities with dead bodies. And certainly the casualties of the occult are predominant among those who approach Christian priests for exorcism.

The activity that causes the greatest repugnance and fear is Satanism, which many feel is growing to unprecedented proportions in both America and in Europe. Some workers have predicted that when Satan worship really gets going, the drug problem will become of minor importance. In 1971 the Church of England had, for the first time, fewer than four hundred new deacons; the number of men training for the Catholic priesthood in England has dropped by a quarter since 1961. Yet in America in 1971, 450 Ministers of Satan were ordained in one week. Anton Szandor La Vey's Church of Satan was founded in 1966 and now reckons to have more than 7,000 members in twenty-five places throughout the United States. La Vey (once Howard Levy of Chicago and a lion tamer) has constructed a detailed liturgy and ritual with a Satanic Bible, programmes for Satanic masses, weddings and funerals, with a wide variety of interesting vestments and artefacts. La Vey's main principle seems to be that since Christianity is dead there is no need to try and embody anti-Christian elements into his forms of worship. Speaking of the end of the black mass, he says: '. . . use of the mass as an inverted magical ritual has declined. If it did not work frontwards, why should it work backwards?'[2]

The Satanic Process Church of the Final Judgement seems at first glance so similar to be La Vey's. Its adherents wear black cloaks, long hair, beards and regard Satan, Lucifer and Jehovah as the 'three gods of the universe'. The leader of the cult claims to be a reincarnation of Christ. The church was founded in London in 1963 but moved to Mexico, then to the States. The sect contains no trace of witchcraft or assonance with the black mass. In fact they are taken quite seriously by a number of people even though they are counter-cultural, pacifist, anti-narcotic and are opposed to the established Churches. The Church is based on a belief in one God of whom Satan, Lucifer and Jehovah symbolize the ways in which man has experienced him.

At one time it was believed there was a link between the Process Church and the sadistic Satanism of Charles Manson and his hate-fear-death commune, but this has been shown in court to be non-existent. Manson and his family, represent another aspect of Satanism, a well-organized and possibly homicidal sect of which there are several in America. Manson's religion seems to have been derived from such sources as Scientology, the Process (Manson also claimed to be a reincarnation of Christ, and his followers sported black capes as well), the Solar Lodge of the Ordo Templi Orientalis, Beatle-mania, all bolstered with a heavy drug scene.

The Solar Lodge of the O.T.O. was another desert commune of individuals who would 'hold magic meetings where they would try to summon and radiate hate-vibrations into the Watts ghetto in order to start riots ...' These sects would certainly come under a definition of black magic — magic used for destructive ends. Satanism, of course, can be defined by demand for a definite oath of allegiance to Satan.

In America the Satanic movement is more evident than it is in England, mainly because it has a more dynamic and publicity conscious leadership. Moreover, while witchcraft in England is not illegal (the witch-craft laws were finally abolished in 1951) publicly known Satanists would certainly find themselves the subject of local abhorrence expressed in positive ways. The English will accept anyone, however odd or perverse their ideas, if they present a modest and conservative image. Consequently England's white witches are quite well-known through television appearances and newspaper interviews.

Nevertheless, there is ample evidence of Satanic or black magical practices in England and the list of churches that have been vandalized or desecrated by Satanists as opposed to wayward hooligans increases each year. The main focus in London is the romantic and grossly neglected Highgate Cemetery where many famous individuals are buried including Karl Marx, who would probably be amused at the mysterious rites practised around his plinth.

These contemporary exhibitions of black magic, with their automatic concomitants of sex and drugs, can seem rather unnerving as well as pathetic. And they have a feeling of viciousness that may well be dangerous to gullible participants. A precedent that is often looked back to in this connection is the famous Hell Fire Club at West Wycombe which flourished towards the end of the eighteenth century. There were several Satanist dens around in England at the time, but basically they seem to be mainly designed for noisy and uninhibited sexual orgies. The atmosphere was always well contrived with elaborate decor and costumes (the girls dressed as nuns) and some gestures were made towards parodying the Roman Catholic rites. The class system of England at that time would have allowed the aristocratic young males to make fairly free use of the local peasant girls.

Occult groups and orders using lengthy ceremonies and involved rituals flourished in the nineteenth century. From this complicated mass of Rosicrucianism and surviving medieval magic, certain familiar names arise, notably those of the poet W. B. Yeats and Aleister Crowley, poet and demoniac prophet. They were associated with the Hermetic Order of the Golden Daw which was responsible for the survival of ritual magic in both England and the United States. Crowley became extremely famous as a black magician and thoroughly enjoyed his reputation. Some of his methods of inducing demonic possession are mentioned in a later chapter.

Crowley died in 1944, the central figure of a minor cult, but to the general public he was a vague, mythical person with a bad reputation. More influential in bringing the messages of the occult to the common reader, and in enticingly accessible form, was the novelist Dennis Wheatley whose well-researched and gripping devilish books became best-sellers. Whether Wheatley, through his work, prompted individuals to explore the occult is debatable. Wheatley himself has called for reinstatement of the witchcraft laws in England. In 1974 a 'black magic' trial caused some publicity; the case involved desecration of graves in Highgate Cemetery, use of a headless corpse and a naked girl dancing on tombstones.

In a radio interview, Dennis Wheatley remarked of black magic and its exponents: 'Nine-tenths of them are phonies. To call down the powers of evil is a life time's job. Most of these people are in it just for sexual orgies and the dope traffic. We should investigate the powers of the human mind, certainly, but this monkeying about with unknown forces is dangerous for the weak-minded. I've known people neglect their wives and families and end up in the loony-bin. The witchcraft laws should be brought back. First offenders should be given a very strict warning, but a second time — then they should be slapped down.'

The more vocal Christians, such as John Richards in England, are showing great concern. The idea of a personal, incarnate devil, or of individual, possessing demons is shrugged aside, and the emphasis placed on feelings, what the hippie is likely to call 'vibes'. Billy Graham remarks: 'There is the all-pervasive, subtle and evil influence of the devil throughout our society', and Dr

Michael Ramsey, the recently retired Archbishop of Canterbury can speak of 'forces of evil of a supernatural kind that sometimes get hold of people'.

Were Hogarth to illustrate the credulity of the late twentieth century he would delightfully include all the tricks of the Age of Aquarius; his barometer of psychosexual disorders could stay, but the books littering the place would be *The Exorcist,* Tom Tryon's *The Other* and Ira Levin's *Rosemary's Baby* which dealt with a girl who believed that she was carrying the child of the devil. (Roman Catholics in some localities were barred by their church from seeing the film of this book, though support was given to the film of *The Exorcist.*) Hogarth would also probably include incense, pot, sexual liberation, bayonets and tear gas, Manson, Hell's Angels, the Satanic churches and a scattering of Tarot cards and yarrow sticks (with which the *I Ching* is read) in one hellish brew with its undertow of extreme violence beneath the surface trivia of ouija boards and crystal-ball gazing, and in a corner, two Jesuit priests fully robed performing an exorcism with holy water and the Roman Ritual.

In this context a revival of interest in exorcism is not surprising, for exorcism represents a unique image and is of compelling interest for both the Christian world and the non-Christian seekers.

For the occultist, exorcism is another facet of his search for communication with spirits: the seance, the ouija board, the psychic sit-in are all attempts to raise a spirit and to him, exorcism comes within this category; that the spirit present must be assumed to be an undesirable one (otherwise why exorcize?) is irrelevant to the sensation of approaching the desired communication.

To the Christian, however, exorcism represents the

one sure weapon with which to fight the influences
of the occult, to restore sanity and reason to the disturbed
individuals who have escaped from covens and cults by
re-incorporating them into a Christian witness. As we
have seen in the previous chapter, Protestant exorcism
methods have always been modest and less spectacular
than the Roman rites. Today Christians must attempt to
rid the ceremony of any vestige of magic. Exorcism must
not be seen, the Christian minister claims, as a form of
'counter-magic' to evil, but as a part of the healing
ministry. Thus exorcism is only a start to what amounts
to a course of therapy involving prayer, communion
and rehabilitation. The age of reason has banished
Asmodeus, Pazuzu, Belphegor, Leviathan and all the
other personalized demons; but the effects once attributed remain constant and when medicine and psychiatry fail, then exorcism raises its head once more —
a new, improved version maybe, but still medieval in its
principle.

5

EXORCISM TODAY

The outburst of interest in exorcism may appear to have been sudden. But in fact fascination for this rare rite has been growing steadily for over a decade. The much publicized book and film, *The Exorcist*, has merely given this interest a precise, if somewhat sensational focus. Since an exorcism consists essentially of a dialogue (albeit acrimonious) with a spirit, it is, as a technique, a natural concomitant with the increasing enthusiasm for the occult. In particular the charismatic movements both in America and Britain have helped to revive the concepts of good and bad spirits. Deliverance through exorcism is commonplace for charismatics who believe that they have been possessed by the Holy Spirit and therefore have the gift of discernment of other spirits, especially demons working in other, troubled, people.

There is an extensive literature devoted to exorcism and to possession. One of the more distinguished books on the subject to appear recently includes a bibliography listing well over 300 individual sources. Some of these books are out of print, a few contain passing references while dealing primarily with other subjects, while others are fairly esoteric essays tucked away in learned theological journals.

But all this clearly indicates that exorcism has never been a dead subject and that there is, in fact, a substantial body of thought (with not a little controversy) related to it. Not all the studies have been made by theologians or fanatical pentecostalists. Doctors, psychiatrists and anthropologists have all made their expert contributions.

In his book *The Manufacture of Madness*, the distinguished American psychologist Thomas S. Szasz writes: 'The change from a religious and moral to a social and medical conceptualization and control of personal conduct affects the entire discipline of psychiatry and allied fields'. Psychiatry, he argues, has today taken over the leading role once occupied in society by the Church, and forms of behaviour once stigmatized by the Church as heresy are now stigmatized by psychiatry as illness. So it is not perhaps surprising that doctors, psychiatrists, and psychotherapists have shown themselves more responsive to the possibilities and implications of possession and exorcism than have priests and theologians who have accepted a demythologization of the devil and his demons — that is, disavowed a literal interpretation of Satan.

One important reason for this has certainly been that in recent years individuals, who have displayed symptoms of what would once have been regarded as demonic possession, have been directed towards the psychiatrist rather than towards the clergyman. And whereas the psychiatrist is likely to have an awareness of the importance of the mind-body link through his study of hysteria and psychosomatic disease, the clergyman will probably confess himself unequipped to handle the physical side of the problem, or perhaps even to see physical symptoms as at all related to a spiritual malaise. But both doctors and psychiatrists have been baffled by certain patients which has made the concept of demonic possession, for some of them at least, a probably reality.

There are dangers attached to a misdirection of therapy. The attentions of a doctor are much less likely to damage a person who is apparently possessed, even though they may be of little positive assistance.

But to bring the suggestive rituals of exorcism to a person who is only physically ill could well cause wholly unnecessary mental distress. And indeed, one might add that the same applies to psychiatry.

One of the great difficulties of conducting an exorcism is the suggestive quality that the ritual has, inasmuch as it frightens the onlookers in a particular way, to the extent that they may feel themselves possessed. When exorcisms were performed in public during the great age of witch-hunts, associative hysteria would often break out among the onlookers, thus making the situation worse.

Today, when an exorcism has to be performed in public — as in the case of the exorcism of a house for example — the officiating clergyman is specifically asked to be as discreet as possible, to avoid drawing casual public attention to what is happening.

The 'scientific' interest in possession shown by doctors and psychiatrists, added to the definite spread of occult practices has forced many priests, and Bishops to re-think their position on exorcism. And here, another point must be emphasized — the important distinction between two sorts of exorcism: Christian and non-Christian.

As I have argued in the chapter on the New Testament demoniacs, the essential function of Christ himself as an exorcist was made an integral part of the whole system of Christianity which has been so aptly described as 'the exorcism of a culture'. Christian exorcism works, then, as the triumph of Christ himself over the evil of the world. The Christian exorcist operates by invoking the power of Christ to bind the possessing demon.

Non-Christian exorcism (that is, in pagan and occult systems) works through the personal power of the exorcist himself. Seen from this point of view, the non-Christian exorcist becomes something akin to an indivudual magician working through his or her own charisma according to whatever occult or religious system both the exorcist and the possessed belong to.

The Christian exorcist, on the other hand, sees his job as a part of the whole ministry of the Christian Church, so that in theory at least all ordained priests and even particularly devout Christian laymen should be able to perform an exorcism, although in practice this is discouraged.

The average parish priest may well find himself embarrassed and at a loss were he asked to perform an exorcism. He would probably agree that in the past the Church did treat cases of mental illness as demonic possession, but feel that was outdated now, and recommend group therapy instead. A reaction probably shared by many is delightfully expressed by John Richards who writes of 'British mistrust of fanaticism coupled with a basic shyness together with a lack of spiritual discipline and the discernment that comes with it . . . ' (Richards makes it quite clear he is speaking only for himself and not generalizing about others).

Faced, however, with urgent or insistent demands, the parish priest is most likely to say a few informal prayers and perhaps celebrate Holy Communion with the troubled person, or in the demon-infested house, rather than indulge in the full ceremonial of exorcism rites. But as one Anglican clergyman has remarked: 'Tea and sympathy exorcisms are of no avail at all'.[1] By this he means that to go along and perform an exorcism and then to go away without any follow-up or after-care of a Christian-spiritual nature, is useless. One is reminded of the attitude of many clergy to people who only approach the Church for marriage.

In 1972 the Church of England made an official statement on exorcism in a report on the subject produced after a commission, convened by the former Bishop of Exeter, had been deliberating for some nine years. The final recommendation of this report suggests that: 'It is much to be desired that every diocesan bishop should appoint a priest as diocesan exorcist, and that in each province, centres of training should be established . . . '

Against the historical background of exorcism, with its dramatic and fearful colouration of neurosis and hysteria (so much of which can now certainly be declared as non-demonic origin) such a suggestion emerging from the enclaves of sober-suited Anglicanism may appear somewhat surprising, if not alarming. The implications of a revival of a whole, nation-wide order of exorcists, together with the need for special training, does tend to indicate a rather unnerving belief that demonic possession is frequent and on the increase.

Within its terms however, the Exorcism report does indicate a perfectly sensible attitude, being a proper and thoughtful response to an increasingly well-stated social theme. As we have seen in the previous chapter, interest in, and active participation in the occult, witchcraft and various satanic practices great and small, is a formidable reality.

And all Christian commentators on the subject insist that, sooner or later, indulgence in such practices will leave the individual mind wide open for the invasion of evil spirits, whether it be schoolchildren having an apparently harmless session with an ouija board during the lunch break, or whether it be a full dress (or undress) black rite in a London cemetery, complete with headless corpses stolen from nearby graves and religious artefacts plundered from the local church.

Now, whether this concept of spirit invasion is to be taken quite literally, or whether the expression is a metaphor for the emotional and mental damage suffered by vulnerable or susceptible minds, or even whether it merely means behaviour not consonant with Christianity (though it may be perfectly proper within the alternative religion or occult system) is not at this point relevant. What is relevant is that the Exorcism report is not implying that the world at large seems to be reverting to a sort of medieval witchcraft consciousness and that therefore the Church too must revive the appropriate weapons of that age with which to combat it. This would indeed be proposing to match superstition with ritual in an isolated, if dramatic, way.

The Bishop of Exeter says as much in his foreword to the report. He was prompted to start work on the subject as long ago as 1963 because, apparently, he himself was inundated with requests to perform exorcisms, and at the same time, the national Press was showing an 'unhealthy and near-hysterical' outburst of interest in the subject. There was a similar manifestation in 1974 when the film *The Exorcist* received such wide publicity. One London Sunday newspaper ran a three-week series on exorcisms and those exorcized, apparently mainly pop-star transfixed school-girls and frustrated housewives.

The impression given, in both resurgences, is that exorcism is a kind of spiritual equivalent to surgery. Just as the appendix or a cyst can be cut out by a trained surgeon, so a troublesome demon may also be 'cut out' as it were, by an expert on the subject. The Bishop describes this conception as 'a purely negative action of expelling an evil force or cleansing an evil environment'.

The temptation to analogize between exorcism and

physical surgery is strong. The most likely sequence of events that charts the course of a bodily illness is: feeling ill, diagnosis, treatment, convalescence, return to a normal, active life as before. Treatment of the possessed may run a similar course as far as the first three stages go — though the symptoms and the diagnosis of demonic possession present infinitely greater problems than those produced by the average physical affliction. For 'treatment' read 'exorcism', but after that the progress must be slightly different. If exorcisms were merely spiritual surgery, then the analogy would be consonant. But the Church's attitude is that if the exorcism is to have any validity at all, a possessed person must be thoughtfully guided towards a truly Christian life-style, and all that that implies. In the case of the possessed, this cannot mean a return to a previous way of life if that involved habits, contacts or influences which may have helped to create the sense of possession.

The space left by the removal of an appendix is not filled up with anything unless the surgeon accidentally leaves his swab inside the patient. But it is endemic to Christian exorcism that the space vacated by the departing demon is filled, and that this in-filling consists of building up a Christian way of life. The Bishop of Exeter writes of it in this way: '[exorcism's] positive aspect as an extension of the frontiers of Christ's kingdom and a demonstration of the power of the resurrection to overcome evil and replace it with good . . . '

As we have already seen, it is a' characteristic of the New Testament exorcisms that the cured demoniacs become converted to Christ and henceforth go about spreading his word. It is, perhaps, worth noting at this point that one of the main reasons why the film *The Exorcist* failed to suggest the true nature of Christian exorcism was because the child, after her cure, was clearly unchanged (apart from being a little pale and wan, as well she might) and her mother, equally clearly had no intention of changing either, but remained a non-believer. This emphasized the magical/superstitious aspect at the expense of theology. In the original novel the child is noted as gazing curiously at the roman collar of a visiting Jesuit priest, again as though it were some magical talisman.

Throughout history the dual function of the exorcist has been to get rid of evil in order to secure good — the good, of course, being consonant with the particular religion of the time and place. The contemporary Christian exorcist is therefore performing the same function as his predecessors in Babylonia, Assyria, ancient Egypt and ancient Greece. But to this must be added an awareness of the evangelical nature of the Christian exorcism — and here we may find a further clue as to why so many leading theologians and the Church itself has taken a renewed interest in the practice. The Bishop of Exeter refers coolly to 'the widespread apostasy from the Christian Faith . . .'

The argument seems to be that if an individual has rejected Christianity and taken up, *in its place,* an alternative religious or occult practice then that individual may well be vulnerable to symptoms of demonic possession. Only a total rejection of the alternative religion accompanied by an uncompromising return to the Christian fold can secure a cure — and exorcism is the highly dramatic turning point. With its quasi-magical use of water, salt, perhaps oil, ecclesiastical robes and holy objects, exorcism is, in the words of Père Joseph de Tonquedec, 'an impressive ceremony, capable of acting effectively on a sick man's subconscious . . .'[2] Even, one might add, on his conscious state as well.

Whether one believes in demonic possession or believes that the symptoms are the result of social-cultural pressures, one thing is certain: when an individual is in such a state that an exorcism is considered necessary he is extremely vulnerable and very open to suggestion. Indeed, one feels that if an exorcism accompanied by such heightened rituals and atmosphere, was conducted in the name of Isis, Shakespeare or Freud, it would have a suitably calming, though possibly temporary, effect.

The Exorcism report was a major attempt to clarify and unify attitudes to the subject. It is a significant document and its history implies some comment on the situation regarding exorcism today. The report was delivered to the bishops in 1964 — but was not actually published until 1972. This time lapse has dated the report in certain ways, but its final publication and general availability revealed a response to a growing need in the 1970s for information and direction on the subject. Several books also appeared about this time, not heavy studies but lively accounts from individuals whose pastoral work had begun to include experience of exorcism or some form of deliverance.

By the time the report was publicly available some bishops had already followed up one of its recommendations — that each diocese should have someone specially trained for exorcism. But until then the Anglican Church seems to have regarded exorcism as very much a question for the personal decision of the priest involved. And, of course, some priests made it their speciality, using their own sometimes informal or intuitive techniques. Also sometimes apparently seeing a need for exorcism in cases where, although the patient is unquestionably troubled, he or she may be suffering more from cultural or social misconception than from an active and external force.

A similar situation applies within the Roman Catholic Church where the separate function of exorcist has virtually disappeared. However, the office of exorcist is one of four minor orders automatically conferred on the ordinand, and incorporates a dual power. One is ordinary exorcism which is applied to handle the concept of temptation, and which is used in the baptismal rites (recently revised to include the restoration of ordinary exorcism prayers). The other form of exorcism, to combat possession, is known as solemn exorcism and its use is restricted to priests specially deputed to the office by the Church. The full instructions and rites are contained in the *Rituale Romanum.*

But again, orthodox or mainstream clergy in the Roman Catholic Church would rather not get involved in these elaborate and genuinely awe-inspiring rituals which they feel should only be brought out in cases of extreme desperation. But there are plenty of freelance exorcists who, like their Protestant counterparts, are ready to leap into action with little premeditation. And when individual exorcists of either Church receive publicity for the more sensational cases in which they might get involved they tend to become a source of embarrassment to their colleagues. Despite the efforts of the Press and the entertainment world, it is no longer fashionable to believe in the devil or in his entourage of demons.

6

A RITE NEITHER SIMPLE NOR POINTLESS

Until it is superseded, or until episcopal guidance is given — something many clergy would appreciate — the Exorcism report will remain the Anglican authority on the subject. As such, it may be regarded as a parallel document to the ancient *Rituale Romanum,* compiled by Pope Urban VIII which is used by the Roman Catholic Church. Each rubric contains similar warnings, conditions and instructions, most notably that the exorcist should be slow to believe that the person presented is in fact possessed by an evil spirit.

Beyond this, however, there is a perceptible difference in tone as the *Rituale Romanum* refers positively to the behaviour of demons and of the devil when an exorcism is taking place. Thus, demons are credited with 'arts and subterfuges', with will and with a tendency to gossip in order to divert the attention of the exorcist.

All of this lends demons the attributes of a factual existence. The Exorcism report does no such thing. Certainly, it implies that exorcism has its dangers, particularly for interested but uncommitted onlookers, and for the patient himself. But these dangers are seen more as emerging from the situation itself, rather than from the actuality of demons.

This is consonant with the predominant Christian view of exorcism which is that, while being of increasing importance to the ministry, exorcism should properly be associated more with the general work of deliverance than with isolated acts directed at 'so-called demonic "possession"', which, the report stresses, is an extremely dubious concept. To this end it reminds the reader that exorcism over human beings 'was a normal, frequent and repeated routine liturgical action for Christian initiations from the end of the second century at least'.

As already mentioned, a prayer of exorcism has been incorporated into the reformed baptismal rite of the Roman Catholic Church — a quite short but impactive prayer. However, should the impression remain that the exorcism rites of the early Church were of a similar, fairly minor emphasis within the context of the initiation ceremonies, it is important to study these solemnities.

In the early Church the conversion of peoples to Christianity was a formidable task. The bishops were working among populations with fully established traditions of different kinds of worship especially in Greece and the mid-east: paganism, sun-worship, fertility cults, homage to the old gods intermingled, and these religions held total sway over the individual and completely influenced the way in which he conducted his life. In our diversified, educated, socially affluent, contemporary society it is perhaps difficult to assimilate this and certainly easy to underestimate it. A modern analogy might be the man whose entire life is governed by the giant corporation in which he is a rising career executive and on which he depends for the plan of his entire life even beyond his retirement.

All these religious systems and forms of worship had their own highly developed cults and rites of initiation which were purposely shrouded in mystery, presumably in order to keep their adherents in a state hovering somewhere between awe and sheer terror. There is some controversy as to whether or not the early Christians merely imitated pagan principles by adapting their rites to the new purpose. Nevertheless these self-same elements of mystery and fear were strongly emphasized and whether calculatedly drawn from paganism or not, the rites were certainly designed to make a similar appeal to the new converts and the Christian mystagogs believed that the stimulation of such responses was to be desired.

About the initiation rites of the early Church, Fr Edward Yarnold S.J. has written:

> The almost daily fasts, the daily instructions and moral exhortations, the repeated exorcisms, the recurrent prayers ... have all conspired to tune (the initiate) to a pitch of excited anticipation ... the procedure seems to be calculated explicitly to stir up emotions of spiritual exaltation and awe, which will help to make of baptism a life-long and profound conversion.

In a footnote to this passage, Fr Yarnold comments: 'In our own century the use of psychological devices to promote a lasting spiritual conversion was familiar to givers of old-style parish missions, and is still employed by the most up-to-date evangelists.'

These early initiation rites are particularly interesting and are described in detail by Fr Yarnold in his book *The Awe-Inspiring Rites of Initiation.* The book includes newly translated and annotated sermons prepared by four fourth century mystagogs which were intended as an explanation to the initiates, of the formalities they had just been through. Acceptance into Christianity was a lengthy and, as indicated, a rather unnerving experience. Ceremonies of exorcism occurred several times, as part of the general preparations and again during the baptism formalities.

At that time all pagans were regarded as being possessed by the devil, so renunciation of his works, followed by protection against his blandishments were important. The mystagogs helpfully listed many of the devil's more treacherous enticements and were particularly severe on sooth-saying, astrology, looking for omens, casting spells and making divinations — all of which were important elements in the religions that the new converts were leaving. Cyril of Jerusalem strikes a positively twentieth century note when writing about the pomps of the devil: ' . . . the mad world of the stage, horse-racing, hunting and all such futility. . . . Do not be keen to set eyes on the madness of the theatre, where you will witness actors indulging in obscenities and outrages and every kind of impropriety, and un-sexed men dancing in abandoned fashion.'

Initiates were given lengthy homilies of introduction, and taught to pray and the meanings of the prayers explained. The rituals involved being stripped completely for the total immersion of baptism, anointing with oil, dressing again in white, then being received by the congregation with joy and introduced to the most solemn and holy mysteries of the mass. All of this was conducted with the maximum of drama. The physical demands and the atmosphere of the ceremonies themselves would be as moving as the emotional impact of the actual words. The rituals were conducted daily throughout Lent. Daily instruction was followed by a visit to the exorcists and — says John Chrysostom — 'this rite is neither a simple one nor a pointless one'.

The specific exorcism rites varied in detail from place to place and from time to time, becoming increasingly more elaborate. The repetition of exorcism over such a lengthy period was explained by the belief that demons are in general only expelled gradually from a person and as the persons faith increases so the area which had been occupied by the demonic influence slowly decreases.

There were two main elements in the exorcism process. The first was the verbal one — that is the expulsion of the devil by a form of words. The initiate was instructed to stand, eyes lowered and in an attitude of prayer, barefoot on sackcloth with his outer garments removed. It is understood that the candidate was asked to face the west which was regarded as the source of darkness and therefore as the dwelling place of the devil.

Vocal denunciations and accusations, these 'marvellous and awesome words', were of major importance. Chrysostom remarks that 'no demon, however fierce and harsh, after these fearful words ... can refrain from flight with all speed'. And they were accompanied by the second element of the exorcism ritual which consisted of various symbolic acts. The semi-nakedness of the candidate symbolized the notion that he was once in the devil's power. The sackcloth, on which he stood, (sometimes it was the fleece of a goat) represented vices and sins which must be trodden underfoot. One frequently used gesture was that of blowing on the devil, using the conventional action of contempt. In later centuries there are references to the candidate spitting on the devil.

Anointment with oil was incorporated into the exorcism rituals. Sometimes the sign of the cross would be traced in oil on the candidate's forehead in order to avert the devil's gaze. On other occasions the whole body would be anointed, a ritual intended to supply the initiate with a source of strength for the ensuing struggle with the devil. Olive oil was used, also chrism — olive oil blended with a scent, balsam usually.

After the day's exorcism routines had been completed, the initiate's face was covered to help him attain peace of mind and to help him from being distracted in his prayers. Penance would be urged as well, through the

wearing of hair shirts and by fasting. The oil used on
these occasions, and the water used in baptism were
themselves exorcized with appropriate prayers and then
filled up with the Holy Spirit.

It should be understood that the candidates for
initiation into Christianity at this time were not suffering from personal demonic possession with its supposed
symptoms of madness and violence. They were merely
considered to be under the dominion of the devil. In
the section on the exorcisms of Christ we found New
Testament justification for the idea of all non-Christians
being already tainted, or corrupted, by satanic influence.
And arguing from the particular to the general the
concept emerged of Christ himself as the exorcist of a
whole culture.

If one sees our contemporary culture as becoming
demonized, for as such the increasing apostasy from the
Christian Church has been described, then in the modern
Church exorcism may well be encouraged to assume a
similar status to that which it held in earlier centuries
— not as an isolated act of emergency, but as a powerful
psychological method of regaining lost congregations.

As we shall see in the next chapter, some individual
ministers who practice exorcism seem to do so on what
appears to be fairly flimsy evidence. Individuals who
are simply worried, distressed and oppressed by social
conditions are offered exorcism as a remedy. (I say
'simply' not with the intention of minimizing their acute
unhappiness which is often approaching a state of
nervous breakdown, but to distinguish it from the
textbook symptoms of demonic attack.) The attitude
of this category of exorcist is probably consonant with
the view that exorcism should be a part of the process
through which a person is accepted into, or rehabilitated
to, the Christian Church.

Through the centuries the nature and function of exorcism in the liturgies changed. Its place as an integral part of Christian initiation continued to be recognized, but it slowly became reduced to a section of the baptismal service. On the other hand the development in the middle ages of a complex and vivacious demonology with a list of named devils each with its own speciality, and the towering figure of a personalized Satan, meant that exorcism emerged as an elaborated tool with which to confront individual demonic possession. After all, even baptized Christians could be subject to demonic attack.

This distinction is clearly recognized today by the Roman Catholic church with its use of an ordinary exorcism as in the baptism service, and of a solemn exorcism for those who are personally possessed. Pre-Reformation practice distinguished four broad categories in which exorcism was applied. These exorcisms took the form of either command to the demons, or a prayer to God for protection from, or release from, their power.

The first category was all candidates for Christian initiation. As we have seen these rites gradually became less elaborate and when infant baptism became the commonly accepted practice they were incorporated into that service. They were retained in the first prayer book of Edward VI (1549) but were later dropped. Specific exorcism prayers were considered unnecessary in countries that had acquired a long Christian tradition, and the same attitude still applies. The Anglican baptism service today includes several passages relating to the renunciation of the devil.

However, even today, where the Christian Church has an outreach in countries that were until recently, or indeed still are, of pagan or primitive persuasion, then exorcism in this general sense still holds a more clearly defined place. Its reaffirmation in the revised Roman baptism rite (1969) suggests that it is needed today even in Christian countries where children may be emerging from the background of a family which is, to all intents and purposes, pagan. Relevant too, is the growing need to help those who are trying to rid themselves of a preoccupation with the occult, or who feel harassed by bad feelings or vibes emanating from certain elements in society as a whole.

The second category was the exorcism of objects such as oil, water, and salt, as well as holy objects, which were to be used in the various rituals of the Church. The third category was the exorcism of places to be used as the sites for churches, or places to be consecrated or re-hallowed. The same impulse is constant, the need to free everything that comes into the church from the domination of the devil.

The fourth category was the exorcism of people other than those who were to be initiated, including, of course, demoniacs and witches. What one might call self-help prayers were employed together with various formulae and devotions used quite naturally by groups or individuals in the course of prayer. Perhaps the most famous is the last petition of the Lord's Prayer: '. . . but deliver us from evil . . .', but there are many other similar phrases of renunciation and invocation in the rituals and prayer books of the Church.

Interesting in this context are what are known as 'breastplate prayers', designed to be self-applied for comfort or protection in an emergency. The best known is that called Saint Patrick's breastplate, and variants of these beautiful, symmetrical hymns are a familiar part of the furniture of domestic Christianity:

Christ be with me; Christ be within me,
Christ before me; Christ behind me,
Christ on my right hand; Christ on my left hand,
Christ above me; Christ beneath me,
    Christ round about me.

Against such a background of constant anxiety about
the devil, and the consequent invocations and prayers
for protection woven so casually and naturally into
the ordinary pattern of devotion, one may wonder how
it was possible for a Christian to become possessed at
all. Much worthy, if refined, argument has been conducted over this point, somewhat on the lines of how
many angels can stand on the head of a pin or how
many children had Lady Macbeth. The fact is, however, that although in theory it might seem unlikely, the experience of several centuries and of the
present age suggests that in practice it is only too
possible.

For this reason, and to deal with this eventuality,
Christian exorcism techniques have been formulated.
In Christian usage the verb 'to exorcize' is applied only
to the demon, and not to the human being or place
possessed. Exorcism commands and binds the evil
within human beings and not the individuals themselves.
The casual expression 'to exorcize someone' is inexact
and should read 'to exorcize over someone'.

Essentially an exorcism consists of the recital of
suitable prayers accompanied by certain actions at
appropriate moments. The prayers may take the form
of a prayer to God to remove the demon, or they may
be directed at the demon. The Exorcism report says
that the earliest exorcism on record consisted simply of
the word '*exi*!' (meaning, *get out*!) which was an
address by a nun to a demon. Whichever form is

chosen, it must incorporate an order to the demon to depart, to harm no one, and — this is essential — to depart to its own place and remain there forever.

One aspect of the Exorcism report that has caused some criticism is its insistence that the actual exorcism should be the end product of a fairly long and painstaking process of examination of the patient, and then after a great deal of careful preparation by the clergyman and assistants involved in the rite.

Ministers and priests who practise forms of exorcism in their day to day work are conscious that many times they are faced with emergencies which have to be dealt with on the spot, and to have to go through the precautionary routines outlined in the report first might mean that their patient could end up mad or even dead through the delay. The report does admit the possibility of 'extreme emergency' but its general tone is that exorcism should really be a last resort.

First of all the illness should be assumed to have a physical or mental cause and the patient should be referred to a psychiatrist by his own doctor. This means that the clergyman will be the last person applied to for help. The report insists that an exorcism should not be performed until all possibilities of physical or mental illness have been completely excluded. But in a later paragraph the report is even more wary. If medical treatment has failed, it says, even then it must not be assumed that the problem has a spiritual source. The limitations of 'psychological medicine' are mentioned. And conversely if medical treatment *is* successful, then there could well be a 'residual spiritual problem' which requires a form of spiritual treatment.

The testing of a person to see if he really is possessed by a demonic spirit, and the decision as to whether exorcism is in order should be undertaken only by a

E

priest with experience in such matters, acting under the
authority of the bishop of the diocese — and usually
licensed by him for the work. These are recommendations,
of course, and as we shall see in the following chapter,
are contested not just by practising exorcists but by
those who see the concept of exorcism in a different
perspective.

Further precautions and delaying actions are apparent
in the system suggested, once exorcism has been decided upon. 'All forms of Christian healing lead the
patient back into full baptismal life', says the report.
And thus emphasis is placed more upon the surrounding
atmosphere of the patient than on the actual exorcism
service. The patient must be trained in the practice of
the Christian life, and 'when the patient is a Christian
and a churchman, regular prayer and confession and
communion should be normal. Frequent laying on of
hands and also, provided the patient is sufficiently
instructed, the administration of holy unction, are
probably advisable as part of healing, and may well
prove to effect the cure rather than exorcism'.

The Church has not, it seems, come so very far from
the general attitudes and approach of the fourth century
to initiates, but consistency may be a virtue. In the case
of unbaptized people needing exorcism, their preparation
must begin from scratch with instruction, preparation
for baptism and, after exorcism, the act of Christian
initiation. These precautions seem to be designed to
prevent charges that the Church is reviving an individual
act of magic, and to suggest that it is responsive to
the knowledge of other disciplines (that is, medicine
and psychiatry) and is being essentially rational. But
from the examples of possession we have already seen
(and those we will mention) it seems improbable that
a person in the grip of what is diagnosed as demonic

possession would have the mental strength, or indeed the will, to follow even the simplest forms of basic Christian instruction.

If it is considered desirable that the patient be as aware as possible of the place of exorcism in the whole symbolism of Christianity and to direct his heart and mind towards the solemnity of the occasion, it is even more important that the officiating priest, or priests, should be in a state of strength and conviction, 'confident of our Lord's victory over evil in general and in the situation confronting him'.

The priest is advised to ask another, experienced in exorcism, to help him in the ritual and that any others present should be mature Christian people who are also sympathetic to this ministry — which probably means that they believe in exorcism; the presence of doubters would, presumably, be as disruptive as the presence of sceptics at a spiritualist seance. The doctor and psychiatrist who have been dealing with the patient should be aware of what is happening, and are invited to attend — if they are mature Christians. However, the number of people present should be kept to a minimum, and those unknown to the priest should not be there, particularly reporters and sight-seers. And the priest is able, at any time, to ask anyone to leave whom he feels is not being of any help. He can also dismiss himself if he suddenly feels dubious or frightened — which is why the presence of a second priest is advised.

Great care is taken with the patient. Exit routes must be closed so that he cannot make a sudden getaway before the service is completed, and he must never be left alone and unattended. The likelihood of violence — either present in the condition, or provoked by the ritual — is accepted and at least two strong men are needed to control a berserk demoniac (and they too should receive suitable spiritual preparation).

These highly realistic provisions are completed by the suggestion that the patient should be seated throughout in a deep armchair. This makes restraint easier, and also means that if the person does fall about he won't hurt himself on the stonework of the church. Exorcism should take place preferably in a church, but if it must happen in a house then children should be removed (after being given a prayer of protection) and also animals. In one recorded domestic exorcism the household's pet dog reacted violently and was later found dead, a possible case of demonic transference.

Taking a cue from Christ's comment that some demons 'only go out by prayer and fasting', the officiating priest is instructed to prepare himself by these means and also help to prepare those who will attend the ceremony by confession, prayer, fasting and communion. It is a good thing too, if the prayers of other Christians, not present, be sought for the general support of all involved.

The service of exorcism is, in itself, fairly short. But a minimum of two hours is recommended in case repetitions of exorcism are required and the devil is only bound for a short time and returns in force after a deceptive period of quiet. Preparations for instant after-care (communion, even baptism) should be in hand in case they are needed.

The preparations made, the appropriate company gathered in the church, the exorcism can begin. First everyone gathers round the seated patient and speaks the Lord's prayer which is followed by a reading of the first fourteen verses of St John's gospel: 'In the beginning was the word, and the word was with God, and the word was God . . .' and silent prayer.

The exorcist then stands before the patient and

delivers the formal command to the demon to depart:

> I command you, every evil spirit, in the Name of
> God the Father Almighty, in the Name of Jesus
> Christ his only Son, and in the Name of the Holy
> Spirit, that harming no one you depart from this
> creature of God, and return to the place appointed
> you, there to remain for ever.

There are several possible variations of this prayer,
notably in the Roman Ritual, the Edward VI prayer
book and the East Syrian Rite. At this point the
exorcist may exhale deeply and sprinkle the patient
with holy water. This exhalation is an ancient method
of invoking the Holy Spirit, and is not to be confused
with the blowing on the devil referred to in the early
initiation rites.

Holy water is made from a mixture of water and salt.
The salt itself is first exorcized and then blessed. The
water, similarly, is first exorcized then blessed. The
two are mixed with a blessing and then this prayer:

> Almighty Father, look with mercy on this creature
> of salt and water and of your loving kindness sanctify
> it. Wherever it shall be sprinkled with the invocation
> of your holy Name may the attacks of evil spirits be
> repelled and the fear of evil be kept far away.

Spirits and demons are supposed not to enjoy the
close presence of consecrated objects, and holy water
is believed to have the property of scalding them. A
belief in the magical properties of salt is ancient and
virtually universal and the respect in which it is held
possibly derives from its qualities of food preservation.
Fr Yarnold quotes John the Deacon writing from Rome
in the sixth century: 'Now that he is a catechumen he
will receive blessed salt, with which he is signed, because

just as all flesh is seasoned and preserved by salt, so too the mind, sodden and soft as it is from the waves of the world, is seasoned by the salt of wisdom and of the preaching of the word of God.' Not only meat then, but persons too can be preserved from corruption. Francoise Strachan[1] reminds us that salt holds a high place in Jewish folklore, being credited with potency; newborn babies were rubbed with salt and this practice still exists in the orient today. And Henry Bouget in his *An Exam of Witches* (1590) writes: 'salt is held in bitter abhorrence by the devil, for salt is a symbol of immortality'. The same writer also refers to the effects of water: 'demons whine and bark like dogs when we sprinkle the bodies of those whom they possess'.

The Exorcism report makes the point that the blessing and preparation of the holy water should be done in the presence of everyone concerned so that they understand that it is a symbol of the prayers and not a piece of Christian magic. And the belief that demons will react to the sprinkling is evident from a note, at this point in the service, that there maybe somewhat violent reactions. If so, the patient must be held down and the exorcism repeated. Here, a breast-plate prayer is recommended, with the exorcist laying both his hands on the person's head. A final prayer and blessing, and the formal ceremony is completed. The report states that it is often useful to renew baptismal promises (if the person has already been baptized in the past), and asserts that if the patient has been involved in occultism then this further gesture is essential.

Christ's statement that when an evil spirit has left a person, it will return in strength if the house has been left empty, implies the need for after-care. The exorcized must be warned of this possibility and encouraged to by all means possible to lead 'a prayerful life in union with the Church, to study Holy Scripture, and to receive the sacraments regularly'.

The Roman Catholic rubrics on exorcism make many similar demands, notably relating to the authority of the priest who is to conduct the ritual. He must be 'properly distinguished for his piety, prudence and integrity of life ... he ought to be of mature years, and revered not alone for his office, but for his moral qualities'. He is urged to study the subject with care, looking into case-histories and doing background research, so that he does not jump to the conclusion that the person is possessed without due care and thought.

In the Acts of the National Synod of Rheims held in 1538 there is the warning that the priest should, moreover, make a detailed study of the life of the possessed person, checking up on his condition, reputation, health and other circumstances and consult second opinions since 'the too credulous are often deceived, and melancholics, lunatics and persons bewitched often declare themselves possessed by the devil, and these people nevertheless are more in need of a doctor than of an exorcist'.

These precautions were aimed at putting a brake on the rampant credulity of priests who tended to think that blasphemy or moral acts of which they could not approve were evidence of evil power at work. The emphasis on looking at the case from all angles is obviously intelligent and strikes a particularly modern note.

The exorcism should take place in a church or other suitable place. If the subject is a woman then several other women of good repute should be present, preferably relatives of the possessed. The emphasis on after-care to prevent the spirit returning is also stressed.

Interesting are the instructions to the exorcist himself.

He must be always on the alert for tricks the demon might play — such as pretending to go away, or diverting the exorcist with jokes, deceptive answers or prophecies of the future. Anything that savours of superstition should be avoided and the medical side of the problem is to be left severely alone, this being the province of a doctor. The exorcist is told to try and find out from the possessed if he has been exorcized before and if so what particular words caused the most damage to the demon. In any case he must watch out for this in his own treatment and if he strikes a sensitive phrase which makes the demon angry, then he must repeat it often.

He is told, too, not to make up his own exorcism forms but to use prayers from Holy Writ and to deliver the commands and prayers in an authoritative voice, with confidence, humility and fervour. A crucifix, holy water, and even relics of saints (if they are suitably cased and protected) may be used in the course of the rite, but the Blessed Sacrament should never be brought near the possessed in case of desecration. If, during exorcism, the individual becomes physically troubled with such things as sudden swellings, marks burning on the skin or acute pains, then the holy water is to be sprinkled on these places. As in the Anglican rubrics, it is recognized that, while the actual form of exorcism may be short, a space of three or four hours should be allowed for the repetition of the ceremony several times.

There is a distinct and colourful note of human wisdom and experience in the Roman ritual; there are plenty of implications of terror and of awe but also a feeling of actuality which seems to derive from personal experience of situations of demonic possession. The Anglican report is, of course, also written from experience but in a different age, an age when the concept of demonic possession has altered somewhat. The demonic element in possession, and the whole question of exorcism seems to be a slight embarrassment to the Christian Church. For having been able, after so many years, to dispose of the devil, the Church now finds itself confronted with a situation in which the devil can only be assumed to have a leading role. As we shall show in the next chapter, many clergymen do practise exorcism and have done so for many years but as the devil has been written out of the Canon Law the act of exorcism has assumed a rather wider application.

7

THIS DANGEROUS MINISTRY

A young soldier suddenly started displaying all the classic symptoms of possession — screaming, writhing, throwing himself onto the ground and, apparently, trying to kill himself. His colleagues held him down while the doctor was summoned. The doctor intuitively felt that the padre would be more helpful but when he arrived he felt out of his depth. However, he made the sign of the cross over the man and said: 'In the name of Jesus Christ I command this thing to come out of you!' Whereupon the soldier recovered his senses, but the padre dropped dead.

This story is related by Christopher Woodward in his book *A Doctor's Faith Holds Fast* and is presented as an example of demonic transference, whereby the demon is expelled from one person only to inhabit the exorcist. Dr Woodward has written a number of books exploring the link between medicine and religious faith and in *Healing Through Faith* remarks that 'many of the cases confined to mental institutions ought not to be there at all, but taken to their churches for the clergy to try and exorcize them and cure them'.

Francoise Strachan in her book *Casting Out The Devils* relates the story of a priest performing an exorcism. 'He laid his hands on the patient in the name of Christ — and woke up half an hour later on the floor!' During the time that he was unconscious the demoniac had committed suicide. Eric Maple tells the story of a sixteenth century exorcism. The expelled demon was particularly upset to be driven from the person he had possessed, more so because the exorcist had not told him where to go. 'Oh — go to the privy', the exorcist told him derisively, which the demon did. However, soon afterwards the exorcist had cause to use that privy and was himself attacked in the rear by the cross demon.

Francoise Strachan also refers to a newspaper reporter who was watching an exorcism and 'was affected to the extent that he vomited and passed out'. All commentators refer at some stage to the extreme danger attendant on exorcism. The person possessed is frequently violent, and will reveal sudden and often quite a disproportionate degree of supernormal strength. Quite frail women have knocked strong men unconscious and children have thrown heavy pieces of furniture about. The possessed may easily damage himself in his writhings. He may attack the exorcist or the witnesses in an indiscriminate way; all rubrics insist that helpers should be around to hold down the demoniac during exorcism ceremonies.

The question of actual transference is more problematical because it presupposes the existence of a mobile entity, or extreme susceptibility on the part of the exorcist himself, rather like an unimmunized doctor dealing with smallpox victims. Many priests do claim to have witnessed such transference though, but not always with the fatal result as in the case of the army padre.

The exorcism accounts recounted in earlier chapters all date from the dark days of superstition. Exorcisms were conducted in an atmosphere of utter security and confidence; there was no possibility of alternative treatment since the idea of a disturbed mind producing hysterical physical symptoms was unknown, and rudimentary medical treatment was considered inappropriate since the Church had all the answers. Life was black and white: there was Christ and there were demons, and that was that.

Consequently we may be justified in imagining that the stories are unique in that, confined by ignorance and repressive attitudes to sex, they could not be repeated today. But as we have seen, although the context has altered, the drama in the foreground is often remarkably similar. A case revealed in England in 1974 bears some interesting resemblances to the sagas of the possessed nuns of the sixteenth and seventeenth centuries, though the modern example is without the morbid religious atmosphere.

A sixteen-year-old girl in the north of England felt herself to be possessed by a dead pop star. He revealed himself to her initially through the medium of an ouija board with which the girl and her friends played. The spirit apparently made sexual suggestions to her and: 'The sexual fantasies became so intense that it took both her friends to hold her down when she became aroused'. The girl screamed what are usually called 'obscenities' and began to believe that the pop star wished her to kill herself so that 'they could be together'. The local vicar was called in and he found the girl unconscious on the floor and one of the other girls began to sing in 'a deep American male voice'. An exorcism was ineffectual and the girl was put into a psychiatric hospital where her condition improved. On her return home, however, the symptoms reappeared and this time the house itself was exorcized and the evil lifted.[1]

The sexual root of the case is as clear as it was in the case of Sister Jeanne des Anges, even to the masturbation and rigid coital fits. Once again we find that external expression given to sexual repression is attributed to outside (i.e. demonic) forces. As G. Rattray Taylor has pointed out 'foul language' is really giving voice to the sexual desires of the unconscious mind. And reaction to this seems to have been identical in both sixteenth century France and twentieth century England for as the teenager's exorcist remarked: 'The longing for the enjoyable side of the evil — a sexual longing — is still with her'.

This example illustrates another feature of modern exorcism, one evident too in the incident of the army padre, namely the unpreparedness of so many ministers when suddenly confronted with the need. The first priest called in by the distressed girl did his best, but failed and eventually called in a colleague whom he felt was more experienced. Since some individuals are going to believe that they need to be exorcized, then ministers are going to be confronted with such situations, and this is an argument that supports the Exorcism report's recommendation that exorcists should be appointed and trained.

Sometimes the validity of exorcism is contested within the Church itself. This was exemplified in a case that received some publicity in America in 1973. A family living near San Francisco was suffering from apparently supernatural phenomena. First evidence was a poltergeist effect — objects being flung haphazardly and dangerously around the house sometimes in several rooms at the same time. Mysterious black shadows flitted around and the couple claimed to have been physically assaulted by demons who tried to choke them. Small fires started spontaneously and objects vanished, only to reappear weeks later, broken. Priests, psychologists and mediums were approached for help and finally a Jesuit priest, the Revd Karl Patzelt was called in. After witnessing the demonic effects himself, Patzelt consulted his archbishop who gave him permission to conduct the Roman ritual.

Patzelt, who had also been equipped with fragments of the Holy Cross itself, conducted the exorcism ritual thirteen times before the trouble cleared up. This episode caused considerable controversy in the Church. Another priest, the Revd Richard Byfield said, that 'using the full rite was like using a twenty inch gun to kill mosquitoes. To think that the Prince of Darkness himself — a one-time archangel — would stoop to petty arson and legerdemain with kitchen knives is trying on the imagination. After all, Satan has such a vaulting pride he defied God.' Poltergeists, he added, were usually attracted to children and can be banished by blessing the home.

Another strong critic was the Revd Peter Riga, a priest at St Mary's College in San Francisco, who deplored the apparent belief 'in the medieval superstition of possession, obsession and devil wizardry'. The devil, he said, is not part of Church beliefs. Patzelt himself said: 'There is value in all of this as it brings out the reality of the devil. If the devil is real then God must be.'

Patzelt, quite correctly, sought his bishop's advice in the case, and received his support and help spiritually, and practically since he was given copies of the appropriate rite in Latin and in English and also the holy relics. But Father Richard Wood, O.P. has suggested that despite a dearth of official exorcisms, in America unofficial exorcisms are increasing. 'Attempts to exorcize the Justice Department and the Pentagon may imply a redefinition of demonic possession in the minds of younger Americans . . .' he adds wryly.[2]

In England too, by no means all exorcisms have been conducted under an official blessing — though one must hasten to add, this observation by no means makes the exorcisms in question somehow either illegal or invalid. Officially, as we have seen, the priest must report back to his bishop on the particular case and receive the bishop's go-ahead and then presumably proceed with the due care and ceremony outlined in the previous chapter.

But as almost every exorcist and every commentator has emphasized, this procedure could be a positive hindrance in the case of emergencies. Fr Christopher Neil-Smith, perhaps the most famous exorcist in England, has described an occasion when he received a telephone call in the early hours of the morning from the wife of an actor who said her husband was going berserk. He went straight round to the house and found a scene of chaos: 'I immediately felt the presence of demonic evil and acted accordingly, making the sign of the cross and praying rapidly for the demon to depart'. This instant remedy was effective and the actor gained immediate relief and was, in fact, never troubled again. But the moral of this particular story — which is by no means unique — is that had Fr Neil-Smith gone through the official routines, the actor might have killed himself or someone else in his convulsive fit before help arrived.

As it happens, Fr Neil-Smith has a licence to practise exorcism granted by the Bishop of London, so he is quite autonomous in his ministry. Other priests who lack both his authority and his experience must, when confronted with such situations, do as best they may. John Richards remarks that at a conference he attended, every person there who was active in the ministry of exorcism had received cases from other ministers who were unsympathetic.[3]

A theological student at Cambridge told me that he was attending, as part of his course, a lecture on exorcism when a fellow student suddenly started shouting, denying Christ and behaving in a possessed manner. The lecturer made the class pray and himself performed an instant exorcism. The student was later, at the insistence of the university authorities, put into a psychiatric unit from whence he returned some time later, 'just normally mad'.

Many clergy do seriously believe that what was once called demonic attack, has in reality a physical or mental (as opposed to spiritual) causation and are therefore unwilling to use exorcism because it seems so like an exercise in magic; conversely, individuals who feel that a priest is the answer to their situation are inhibited from approaching them for the same reason. It seems then that the medical/psychiatric profession on the one hand, and the clergy on the other might try to bridge the gap between categorizations. This is being done in certain areas. Dr Christopher Woodward says that many doctors are coming to accept the fact that there are a group of conditions quite different from paranoia or schizophrenia which are due to outside entities. These he defines as, among other things, temper, spite, jealousy, lust, violence, noise, black magic, sexual perversion and hallucination. From the other side John Richards in his book *But Deliver Us From Evil* recommends that the idea of exorcism be removed from its special province as an individual rite, and its basic meaning brought into the idea of deliverance, or healing through the Church in the widest possible way.

As I mentioned in the introduction, in the popular imagination (as reflected in newspapers and magazines) it is the exorcist himself who commands awe and fear rather than either the victim of possession or the indwelling demon. The exorcist, whether he likes it or not, combines in his image all the mystical qualities of priest and magician. The simple clergyman, friendly and full of faith, will not do; the exorcist must be entirely charismatic.

The non-Christian exorcist who works in the context

of occult and magic groups is closer to the traditional magician and probably sees himself as something akin to the first card in the major arcana of the Tarot pack, complete with cosmic lemniscate over his head, willing earth's forces to be subservient to him. For the non-Christian exorcist works on a demonstration of personal power.

A Christian exorcist, on the other hand, works through the power of Christ which has been given to him just as Christ gave his first disciples power to expel devils and cure diseases. But traditionally he must possess certain particular qualities that do set him apart from his brethren, notably as the Roman rubric states at the outset 'mature years' and he should be revered for his piety. In other words he should project a feeling of authority. He should also be strong, to be able to withstand possible attack from the demoniac and also capable of maintaining the stamina required for what could turn out to be several hours of highly concentrated prayer during a lengthy demonic siege; in some cases exorcisms have been known to go on for days, even weeks. F. X. Maquart has written: 'It is only to priests whose high moral worth protects them from all danger, and whose knowledge and judgement enable them to make a sure estimate of the case put before them, that the Church entrusts the dangerous task of pitting themselves against the devil'.[4] If exorcism is to be seen in such terms as a cosmic struggle then the exorcist is indeed going to display superhuman attributes. 'The more successful the exorcisms the sooner the exorcist dies', is another expression sometimes used. The suggestion that battling·continually with demonic force is draining to the mind and body is a frightening one, though recorded proof of the idea is difficult to find.

Although there is, as we have seen, a specific service

of exorcism in the Protestant and Roman Catholic faiths, not every minister feels automatically able to conduct it; it is not there just to be used when necessary as for example the marriage service. There does seem to be a special kind of vocation which will turn a priest towards exorcism as his own speciality. Some men are particularly good at exorcizing places; others are better with people. John Richards has suggested that there is an almost equal division of responsibility here.

Perhaps the most certain part of an exorcist's personal charisma is brought into play at the moment he makes the decision to conduct an exorcism. Just as most clients who approach a psychiatrist have a diagnostic analysis first, so those who present themselves for exorcism have to satisfy the minister that this is the correct procedure. Many priests do not even consider the possibility and send the patient at once to a psychiatrist. Others do not, and make a careful assessment of their own.

Some exorcists are clairvoyant and can see what is wrong; 'he is able to see what form the entity has taken, and where it is lodged in the patient's physical body or aura surrounding it' writes Francoise Strachan. Some work from experiencing a definite physical sensation. Fr Neil-Smith has described his own approach in his book *The Exorcist and the Possessed*. He describes how when he was practising the ministry of laying on hands he became affected by evil influences and was exorcized by the late Fr Gilbert Shaw. 'It was then, that I was in fact "saved to serve" ' he writes. 'I had to be quite clear that if I was to be of any value as an exorcist, that my own sense of perception must be completely dulled, and what I discerned or diagnosed in people whom I interviewed was the evil force picked up from them and not my own imagination.'

Fr Neil-Smith discerns by vibrations; a vibration which

reveals an evil force is perceived by a sharp sting ('By the pricking of my thumbs, something wicked this way comes', he quotes *Macbeth*) and a vibration that indicates a good force is a gentle tingling. He says that an earthbound spirit gives a heavy vibration and that a demon has an unpleasant cold sensation — a drop in temperature of the room in which the possessed person lies has always been regarded as a sure sign of the presence of the devil. Vibrations felt during an exorcism are like 'the rushing mighty wind' of the Pentecost and some entities with which he has been confronted emit a particularly nasty smell. Another exorcist says he can actually see the entity in the person's body.

It is particularly interesting that Fr Neil-Smith insists that he has to be sure that all the vibrations he feels emanate from the patient and not from his own imagination. Detachment is important. Francoise Strachan recounts an instance in which a lonely woman faked possession in order to maintain the interest of the priest and his assistants, because she enjoyed the attention. Instead of realizing this, the priest, who was himself in a similar situation and needed to be depended upon, became addicted to the idea of regular exorcisms.

Exorcism is a male-dominated world and there are no historical records of female exorcists, though there may have been in the pagan and mystery cults of the ancient world. This is, of course, because women have not until recently, been able to take any active part in the ministry of the Church. The continual emphasis in exorcism on conflict, struggle, battle might also have suggested to possible female exorcists that the feat may be beyond their physical strength.

Francoise Strachan refers to one example in which a possessed woman had defeated the attempts of several male exorcists but was finally cleared by two dedicated female church workers through discussion and prayer. 'In this particular instance the entity fed on the particular vibrations of the previous male exorcists (probably a form of sex magnetism) but was not able to do so with the two ladies', Francoise Strachan comments mysteriously.

Exorcism is not necessarily an art that is confined solely to the priest: laymen (and women) can be successful also. 'I shall never understand, writes Dr Woodward, 'why the clergy and bishops think they have a monopoly over the right to exorcize, it is not even scriptural to presume that . . .'. Tertullian remarked that any Christian who cannot exorcize should be put to death and though they do not advocate such an extreme penalty, many present day ministers share the view that exorcism is not a special gift and is not vocational, but when used correctly — which in their terms means as part of the ministry of Christianity — can be practised by others as well. John Richards in this context comments: 'I wonder whether authority has not only to be *given,* but *received* and *used* before it becomes real?' The Catholic view is that solemn exorcisms are performed in church and that priests alone can undertake them, but that private exorcisms are permitted to the laity. Fr Neil-Smith points out, however, that there are certain cases where an ordained priest speaking in the name of Christ and with the authority of his Church is essential. He is referring particularly to exorcisms of witches who would only recognize a priest of the Church as an equivalent authority to her own high priest, which a layman could not command.

Exorcism is not, as we know, the exclusive property of the orthodox Churches but is practised to varying degrees in occult, esoteric and magical circles. Some of these orders seem quite harmless and indeed somewhat romantic cults with elaborate, operatic rituals.

Others have more definite spiritual aims and there are numerous amateur groups springing up composed particularly of young people who find them a source of drug supply or sexual outlet.

Occultists are almost as rigid and authoritarian about exorcism as the Church, going to great lengths to express the dangers of the rites. There are as many different methods as there are cults. Some pagan witches use hypnosis for exorcism since they understand that the problems presented by the troubled person are usually in the nature of psychological traumas caused by some definite experience. Hypnosis is used to discover the experience and then to erase the memory. Sometimes a person can be hypnotized into altering his pattern of behaviour and thus avoid the circumstances that have promoted an outburst of violence or hysteria.

Ray Buckland, the American authority on the occult and witchcraft uses a system almost identical to that of the Church with incense, salt, water, and certain forms of words.[5] Another witch goes into a trance himself and claims to meet the possessing entities on an astral plane. 'Magical weapons, swords, ritual implements, altars and chalices are simply the means to stimulate the inner self to action and to produce the right atmosphere for a ritual', observes Francoise Strachan. She adds that a group of advanced magicians would need no such supportive artefacts but could achieve the right atmosphere from their minds.

The world of magic does have one special implement that is used in exorcism. It is called the Trident of Paracelsus and consists of a sort of squat pitchfork, magnetized, with a wooden handle. It is used to pierce and exterminate the entities as they materialize. If the exorcist cannot see them, then he stabs about with his trident in the aura of the person. If the demons are very tiny then lots of jabs are necessary; if the demons are very big they will need to be stabbed several times. Demons cannot see the exorcist, but they can see the points of the trident. Some people in England and America take the use of this implement very seriously.

It is impossible to estimate how many exorcisms take place at the present moment. Fr Christopher Neil-Smith has been performing about 500 a year for more than four years. He has performed them in emergency, after deliberation, on television and even over the telephone. Monsignor Luigi Novarese the official exorcist for Rome estimates that he has exorcized about sixty people during his twenty-seven year career. Another Roman Catholic exorcist of the order of the Servants of Mary in the Church of the Seven Founder Saints claims that his exorcisms have run into hundreds.

Since the Exorcism report appeared in England many diocesan bishops have appointed official exorcists who have been finding opportunities to do this work. In the guarded field of the occult and magic, both the raising and the expelling of the devil is frequently attempted.

Fr Neil-Smith's record is exceptional; but then he seems to be an exceptional person. It is quite clear from his writings that he takes a particularly broad view of what constitutes possession, and therefore seems to exorcize many individuals to whom other ministers would prefer giving Christian counselling.

The concept of possession and exorcism is not really a part of contemporary Jewish theology. This is because, being a monotheistic religion the idea of a Satanic force cannot exist. Judaism does, however, recognize one form of possession that is not connected with the idea of a specifically evil opposition to mankind. It is bound in with the idea of transmigration of souls in which the souls of the dead may enter the souls of the living. These souls are called *dybbuks* and are often presented in popular folklore as mischievous and puckish rather than malevolent. The popular writer Isaac Bashevis Singer has featured *dybbuks* in his stories.

The theory is that *dybbuk* possession takes place because the soul is trying to accomplish something it failed to do in its lifetime. Alternatively it may be trying to redeem the evil in the soul it is possessing and therefore should be regarded as benevolent. The Talmud says: 'The person who is afraid of his own unethical and irreligious life is afraid of demons', and consequently instructions to those who considered themselves possessed would be to try and resume a morally pure life.

The principle behind this view is shared by followers of the Islamic and Buddhist religions where there is no modern credence for demons and the feeling is that possession must have a psychological or perhaps physical causation, but that counselling the disturbed person from a point of view of his own religion might be helpful.

Basically this seems to be the situation many people would prefer to see prevailing in the Anglican Church; the overtones of magic that are inevitably present in the formal exorcism rites are, in some quarters, something of an embarrassment. Few ministers reject outright the view that the majority of cases of possession are in fact cases of a disturbed mind based upon what might be called social, or even cultural, oppressions. But the Church will see these things as being due in themselves to a dereliction of Christian principles. Therefore the Church might be more relevant to the curing process than the psychiatrist. But as long as the belief in actual discarnate entities and in evil as an objective influence remains, the exorcism rites will also.

Magic circles meanwhile will continue to chase their own tridents.

NOT ENTIRELY SANE OR SOBER

In this book, the term 'possession' has been used to indicate, specifically, 'demonic possession' which is an experience that is damaging, dangerous and undesirable. But demonic possession is only one aspect — it might be called the dark side — of a phenomenon that is as old as creative man. Throughout history and in all cultures, gods, devils, spirits, demons and various discarnate entities have been believed to enter the human body and take control of the personality. Their number is indeed legion. Possession by the god, or by a holy spirit, has been regarded as the highest and most valuable experience a man might enjoy, and such possession has been actively sought. This sensation is by no means rare today; it happens in semi-primitive societies, in certain cults and can also be seen in the pentecostal movement which received a new lease of life in the late 1960s.

The outward and visible signs of possession are commonly described as madness — a colloquial term, which has no place in the scientific terminology of psychologists. Possession has been variously described as ecstasy, hysteria, enthusiasm, mania. And in this context it is interesting to note that a characteristic of this state has always been giddiness, a word that derives from the old English word *gidig,* which itself meant possessed by the god.

It is possible to chart the course of the possessed state — irrespective of the supposed cause. It is a state that can last for a few hours or for several weeks; in the case of what is called demonic possession the state may recur for years or for a person's lifetime.

First there is a withdrawal from ordinary 'sane' behaviour, which might be involuntary or induced, leading to the onset of actions and attitudes, accompanied by all kinds of physical changes totally at variance with the known character of the possessed and of the standards of the society in which he or she lives. This is a kind of trance state; the person has no responsibility for his actions and afterwards remembers nothing about them. This state will reach a crescendo of activity, including in demonic forms, extreme violence. Then climax of some kind will be achieved followed by a complete relapse, unconsciousness and possibly recuperative sleep. The person will then wake up and resume his 'normal' persona while those who have witnessed the spectacle will either be awed, if it is a god that has been present, or scared to death if the devil has paid a visit.

It will be noticed that this behaviour-graph describes basically the course of an epileptic fit, and also the experience of sexual orgasm — both of which are relevant in any discussion of possession. The main difference between possession by a god and demonic possession is that the former is induced, predicted and controlled: it has a beginning a middle and an end. The latter, however, is not induced; it is unpredictable and extremely difficult to control. Exorcism was the main method of control used for centuries with varying success, and today drug and electrical therapy are used. (At the risk of confusion it should be noted that in the final analysis even demonic possession is in fact induced, though at a deeply subconscious level as we shall see.)

Until the dawn of the age of psychology and psychiatry, these trance-like, ecstatic states were invariably associated with religious practices and worship.

To place responsibility for such behaviour onto the gods (or the devil) absolves man from blame. Today the inclination is to shift responsibility onto social factors thus involving men rather than gods. And religion is seen to be just another element of social pathology like over-crowding, repression, alienation and depersonalization, all of which help to create forms of madness and trauma.

Explanations rob life of its mystery, and a sense of profound mystery has always been at the heart of religion, whatever form it may have taken. In the earliest phases of religious development this feeling alone was the sum total of the experience; it was there — deep, palpable, but at the same time dispersed and inexplicable. Later, man made his first attempts to personalize this mystery, to lend it will and feeling and give it a name. First spirits are projected, later a deity. These creations which man has projected from his own unconscious are given behaviour patterns based on the only available model, man's own behaviour. Hence the pantheon of Greek gods, each representing one aspect of man's character: anger; the pursuit of knowledge; the love of peace; the enjoyment of drink etc. In this way inexplicable behaviour came to be attributed to the action of the gods who had achieved a position of independence and control. Thus when a person behaved in a manner contrary to his normal pattern, or contrary to the accepted social pattern, and when there appeared to be no rational cause for this behaviour and the person was seen to have no control over his actions, the Greeks explained it as possession by the god.

The word demon derives from the Greek *daimon* which means a spirit. But the spirit could force the man into desirable or undesirable behaviour. The Latin form is *genius* which is commonly used today to describe the force behind great creators like Mozart or Leonardo. We do accept the idea of the same force motivating a person such as Hitler, only we make a distinction by calling it an *evil* genius. So, for the Greeks, epilepsy, falling in love and insanity were all due to the same cause: possession by the god. Plato wrote: 'The greatest blessings come to us through madness, when it is sent as a gift of the gods'.

A number of words which we use in a casually devalued way today come from the Greeks' precise definitions of divine states. Enthusiasm, for example, meant the state of a man who knew that the god dwelt within him; ecstasy indicated a sense of standing outside hence the phrase 'he was beside himself'. But all the emotions and reactions thus described were attributed to the god, and not to the spontaneous reactions of man himself. And we find here a distinction between sex (a physical and sometimes sacred act) and love (an inexplicable feeling, gift of the god) which appalled the early Christians who then spent several hundred years welding the two together.

Experience of the god was, of course, to be cherished and men have frequently taken active steps to seek it. All kinds of methods have been used — and still are — to induce the trance-like, ecstatic state of possession which might give the individual magical insights, a knowledge of the future, superior wisdom or abilities. And the Greeks, again, can give us a model example in the rites attached to the worship of Dionysus.

This cult had its genesis in a two-yearly event in Thrace when people rushed off to the mountains to dance wildly to their primitive instruments and to conclude the evening's entertainment with uninhibited, and probably indiscriminate, sex. This eventually became personalized into the figure of Dionysus who was first worshipped by small, exclusive, and possibly all-female, groups but the event was later made available to everyone.

Dionysus was the god of wine and his son Priapus of sexual desire — two things not designed to endear the cult to the Christian outlook. Nevertheless, the purpose was certainly to induce an experience of a transforming religious nature. Dionysus was regarded as the god of healing and the god of joy; Euripides, whose drama didn't exactly glamourize the bacchae, called the rites a method of making cares cease. Plato, sounding like a contemporary psychiatrist says 'they cured anxiety feelings and phobias arising from some morbid mental condition'.

The techniques used in the Dionysian celebrations to induce a sense of possession by the god are precisely those which have been used in all cultures and in all ages from pre-Colombian America to medieval France, from Finland to Mexico: music, dancing, physical exercise, alcohol (or another form of drug) and sex. Additionally, control and concentration have been helped by atmospheric means — use of incense for example, the wearing of clothes appropriate to the group and the employment of suitable talismans and objects which in themselves have no magical property but simply create the needed sense of exclusiveness or apartness.

The effects of all these techniques can lead to results approximating to madness (music itself may lead to a simple trance state and is therefore used to promote dancing rather than for passive listening) but they have always been used within a controlled situation, and this applies particularly to the religious use of drugs. Francis Huxley has pointed out that one of the reasons that modern society considers it has a 'drug problem' is because these ritual bounds and spiritual objectives are missing and the addict becomes attached simply to the idea of being possessed by the drug rather than for any beneficial effects that drug might have.[1]

The religious use of drugs is closely associated with shamanism. The shaman is a sorcerer-priest and is found in cultures all over the world: in Finland, Siberia, central America, south-east Asia. Traditionally shamanism is a hereditary calling and the training begins when the individual is a child. It is a rigorous regime involving singing, dancing, long periods of silent meditation and in fact a conscious cultivation of a kind of behaviour that we would probably call psychopathic. In spirit, the shaman explores the heavens and the regions of hell; he is in constant communication with the spirits and is seer, healer and priest in one.

Not surprisingly, the shaman's mental balance is a delicate one; he is likely to lose control very easily with many 'demonic' manifestations such as bulging eyes, hideous facial contortions, screaming, foaming at the mouth and writhing on the ground. After such an outburst, his people will regard such a man as divinely possessed and in contact with the spirit world. Sometimes people not called to shamanism by hereditary factors adopt the technique probably as a means of externalizing various internal conflicts or frustrated ambitions they may have. It is a calling open to abuse and today a number of so-called shamans are certainly fakes intending to impress sophisticated visitors.

The shaman has always employed the widest range of drugs available to him in whatever part of the world he operates. All over the Americas, for example, tobacco was used along with the leaf of the mate plant, a shrub that contains caffeine. On the face of it, both agents seem to us pretty harmless since tea and cigarettes are hardly conducive to divine trances, but when incorporated into carefully cultivated rituals an effect would be felt, although it might be primarily caused by psychological factors. Tobacco was smoked in very large amounts and when combined with special deep breathing techniques, provided that sense of *gidig* not unfamiliar to heavy smokers today. Well-known hallucinogenic, psychotropic, psychedelic drugs include the peyote cactus (which contains something similar to LSD), marijuana, the datura leaf, the soma plant (believed to be that beautiful mushroom the *amanita muscaria* which is quite dangerous), laudanum and opium. Today of course, manmade drugs are used, notably LSD and forms of tranquilizers and boosters.

If, in Aldous Huxley's phrase, drugs can open the doors of perception, then that perception must be seized and used, which is what the shaman would try to do; to let his mind dive off and seek a new sort of consciousness. Shamans were almost always men, though women have been known to seek the experience. They were always in control of the spirits and never possessed by them.

Another example of a spirit-cult involving a controlled search for possession is in Voodoo, a word itself coming from *vodun* which means god or spirit in the Fon language of West Africa. The Voodoo ceremonies of Haiti involve many trance-inducing techniques — drumming chanting and dancing that may continue for considerable periods of time. The function is for one or more of the worshippers to become possessed by a *loa* — that is, one of the spirits. Most of these come from Africa and African gods are mostly helpful and kind, but there are devil gods and snake gods whose actions are less sociable.

The interesting thing about Voodoo possession is that all the various *loa* are recognizable to the worshippers and each behaves in an expected way. Thus, when an individual is possessed, the onlookers will know which god is in charge. Possession is called 'mounting' and the subject is 'ridden' by the spirit. The sign of possession is when the person's feet stick to the ground keeping him or her immobile while the god enters or mounts, the mind. The person will then behave in character which will be mainly rational. In her book *The Divine Horsemen,* Maya Deren an American film-maker who visited Haiti and became involved in the Voodoo rites, has described how she herself was possessed on several occasions. She called the experience a 'white darkness' and the *loa* that possessed her was Erzulie, the Haitian version of Venus which meant that her behaviour in trance was that of a beautiful, desired and flirtatious woman, distant with the girls but fulsome with the men.

Individuals have no recollection of their behaviour when the spirit leaves them, and though the priest may tell the person which *loa* appeared it is not etiquette to give details of how he or she actually behaved. The period of devine possession can last more than three hours and at any time the priest is able to come between the spirit and the person, even banish it, if the spirit is behaving badly or forcing its temporary body to dangerous or anti-social behaviour.

This scenario bears a remarkable resemblance to a form of spirit possession found in Ethiopia. Again, the spirits — called zars — are given human attributes even to the extent of owning property and having professions. They are believed to have derived from devil-worship but are not necessarily malignant, just a nuisance when they happen to possess a human being.

Again we find the riding imagery as the possessed

person is referred to as a 'horse', the zar making him (or, in this case more usually, her) behave like a horse and produce wild chanting. The priest, or doctor is asked to perform what amounts to an exorcism. He himself is zar-possessed and, going into a trance, calls down his own zar and so is able to negotiate with that of the patient. A promise of gifts is usually enough to expel the zar — a suitable method presumably for a humanoid, property-owning spirit. As happens in Voodoo possession, the victim will go through a range of actions appropriate to his particular zar and afterwards has no recollection of the actual experience. A major difference from the Voodoo practice, is that zar-possession is not solicited.

It has been said that the spirits never visit the entirely sane or the entirely sober, and one would imagine that above all things, a Christian congregation would pride itself on its sanity and sobriety. At least those congregations adherent to the rather dour Protestant ethic. But Christianity has produced its fair share of bizarre behaviour consonant with that produced by spirit-possession in non-Christian religions, as witnessed by the extraordinary behaviour of the early Christian saints whose activities (or lack of them) in the deserts brought them so close to divine possession. Saints and martyrs like Joan of Arc have heard voices and entered trance states, made prophecies and seen visions.

During the eighteenth century, spirit-possession was familiar at revivalist meetings. During the revival in Massachusetts in 1735—42 fainting, falling about, shrieking and trembling were all stimulated under preachers like James Davenport. In England, John Wesley was an impassioned preacher, well able to recreate the terrors of hell that awaited the unrepentant. He recorded several examples of the sensational effects he achieved

F

and these were most often confined to the more illiterate members of his congregations. Raving, whole congregations bursting into spontaneous weeping and wholesale fainting were among the reactions.

Some people went blind and in the three years following 1739 he recorded fourteen cases of temporary insanity and nine incurable ones. At first Wesley assumed that the effects he was creating were due to the Holy Spirit, but later he began to wonder whether the devil was abroad in the air and he started to change his techniques and to discourage the enthusiasm and so the dramatic manifestations disappeared from Methodism. Later in the century there was another revival, this time in Kentucky where under the hell-fire preaching of the McGee brothers and James McGready, outbreaks of jerking, dancing and even barking occurred.

Not dissimilar are the manifestations among congregations in the Pentecostal Church. Although less dramatic today when many pentecostal groups have tended to conform to more orthodox forms of worship, it is still possible to find in Britain and America such things as weeping, fainting and groaning. This movement began in a small bible school called Bethel College in Topeka, Kansas in 1901. Central to the belief is the conviction that baptism by the Holy Spirit is revealed in some ecstatic and preferably dramatic way, mainly by an outburst of glossolalia ('speaking in tongues'), which is an accepted feature of demonic possession and also a feature of the performances of shamans and zar-possessed exorcists. What it seems to mean is that the individual suddenly starts to spout gibberish, or perhaps a distorted form of a modern or ancient language. A number of pentecostalists assumed that this manifestation of the baptism by the Holy Spirit meant that they had been divinely called to serve as missionaries in remote parts of the world because they had been given the linguistic ability. Some did not discover they were mistaken until they got there.

In the last few years a number of new groups have appeared which, while not connected with pentecostalism in the traditional sense, experience speaking in tongues, and believe in baptism by the Holy Spirit, and accept the fundamentalist view of the Bible. This charismatic, or renewal movement is particularly strong in America and has attracted both Catholics and Anglicans. Emotionally oriented movements tend to attract the least educated and most socially deprived sections of society. They offer emotional and reassuring situations for those who feel they have been rejected by, or have no place in, wider society and are therefore the less privileged groups.

Even sex has found its way into revivalism. William Sargant reminds us that in its cruder forms, American revivalism actually encouraged the worshippers to 'come through' to Jesus sexually.[2] If such an orgasm occurred then it was taken as a sign that the Holy Ghost had entered that person's life. Sexual activity increases suggestibility and makes the implantation of belief easier. Dr Sargant adds: 'Repeatedly induced orgasmic collapse has been used to produce states of deep hysterical trance. Further, the implantation of confirmation of religious faith by techniques of this sort is often more effectively achieved in groups than by people in pairs or alone, hence the orgy as a religious rite.' It has also been suggested that the orgy as a religious activity represents a celebration of instinctive drives that are consciously and rigidly controlled at other times.

As we have noted the pattern of sexual orgasm follows the classic pattern of possession. In orgasm both men and women achieve a state akin to possession,

uncontrolled and uncontrollable with accompaniments
of groaning and crying out. This high state of brain
activity is followed by nervous collapse and temporary
inhibition. In view of this, there is little wonder that
individuals have experimented with various sexual techniques to induce a sense of possession.

The tantric cults of India used sexual intercourse to
strengthen religious feeling, and as we have seen the
rites of Dionysus in ancient Greece had an integral
sexuality about them. An urge so basic, and one whose
effects are so accessible to virtually everyone must
have retained forms of expression in Europe throughout
the centuries of severe sexual oppression by Christianity.
The charge of group sexual practices was one often
levelled at witches. Whether this was true because
witch covens were remnants of sexual worship driven
underground by the Church, or because the Church
equated sexual activity in many cases with heresy and
witchcraft being heresy, the two were thrown together,
is very difficult to determine.

Today, sexual aids to achieving either a sense of
possession or at least a trance-like, receptive state,
seem to be confined to small esoteric or witch cults
and groups. William Sargant revealed something of the
extent to which Aleister Crowley experimented with
sexual magic and more about this can be found in
his now published diaries. Crowley used men and
women in his experiments; athletic activity and fasting
were used to prepare the candidate who was then
exhausted sexually by every known means. Crowley
wrote: 'Ordinary acts of love attract or create discarnate
human spirits. Other (abnormal) sexual acts involving
emission of semen therefore attract or excite other
spirits, incomplete and therefore evil. ... Nocturnal
pollutions bring succubi. ... Voluntary sterile acts

create demons, and (if done with concentration and magical intention) such demons may subserve that intention.'

Contrary to popular belief, however, such inventive sexual activity is not necessarily practised in occult and esoteric circles today. Some cells take a positively puritan attitude to sex (their minds are on higher things) while others use nudity, but without any particularly sexual connotation rather like some encounter groups may do.

Divine possession; demonic possession. So often circumstances and symptoms coincide. The difference lies in the perception that an evil spirit or force is responsible for the demonic variety (setting aside for a moment the fact that demonic possession can be ugly, destructive and frightening). But evil depends on the particular perspective of the world and the moves of the relevant culture. Thus to the ancient Egyptian a snake-bite would indicate a malevolent spirit of evil. Today we do not regard snakes as intrinsically evil and we understand the physical nature of poison.

Throughout the centuries the definition of demonic possession has altered and narrowed. In pre-Christian times, apart from the ecstatic symptoms discussed, diseases of all kinds were attributed to demons working within the human body. At these times the definition of demonic possession was probably at its widest.

For the Christian, the demoniacs of the New Testament brought about a new and narrower definition. One important symptom common to these cases, which makes them unique, is that the possessed individuals all recognized Christ without foreknowledge. Even today some theologians argue that demonic possession existed only during the lifetime of Christ, basing their argument on this observation. Most people prefer to alter this symptom slightly to mean that the demoniac recognizes the presence of Christ, that is, in someone else who is a Christian. The typical New Testament demoniac is known by his peers to be disturbed, he recognizes Christ and (through the indwelling demon) cries out to him. Christ demands that the demon leave. The man convulses, faints, then wakes up later cured.

The assassination of Mrs Alberta King, the mother of Martin Luther King, in 1974, happened in circumstances that bear a striking resemblance to Christ's confrontation with the Capernaum demoniac. Mrs King was playing the organ at a church service and after the service had been underway for about ten minutes, and the congregation was reciting the Lord's Prayer, a young man 'rose and started shouting'. According to a report in *The Times* (London) he was overpowered, but not until he had fired his revolver several times, killing Mrs King and wounding others.

A witness said that the man 'appeared to be in a fever' and that the man had come into the church 'to get his enemies'. He shouted that 'all Christians are my enemies'. The structure of this incident conforms exactly to New Testament examples: an awareness of the presence of God, the delirium, the urge to fight against, repudiate the power of Christ. One wonders what the result would have been had the Capernaum demoniac carried a gun.

The history of contemporary American is punctuated with wayward assassinations of public figures usually by individuals working alone rather than as agents of a wider conspiracy. We shall never know whether in this particular case, and in the others, where the motives of the assassinators have lain. But certainly, modern society just as much as those of medieval times, or even gospel times, oppresses certain people and forces them to behave in a way which can only reasonably be attributed to malignant external forces. Since the incident was actually set in a church, the assassination of Mrs King has this particular interest.

The cases of possession and exorcism in the New Testament are, therefore, clearly defined; they have a pattern. As we have seen, Christ distinguished between those people who were ordinarily ill and those who had been bound by Satan. Had the church stuck by this seminal information and applied the rules supplied by the gospels to future cases of possession, then life might have been a lot easier for many people. But in its urge to dub everything non-Christian automatically of the devil, the range of demonic possibility was extended far beyond the limits suggested by the example of Christ's methods and attitudes.

By the fifteenth century, symptoms of psycho-sexual neurosis had begun to appear, thus complicating the issue considerably. But sex was not always the cause of possession; some examples still seem to have a completely inexplicable causation. One such was the outbreak of dancing mania with afflicted the German town of Aachen in 1374. In July of that year a group of men and women described as almost entirely of the poorer classes began to enjoy elaborate hallucinations accompanied by convulsive running, leaping and dancing. Those affected were unable to stop and the fits were only arrested by either force or physical exhaustion.

Quite soon, similar outbreaks were being reported from Liege in Belgium and Utrecht in Holland. Officially the cause was given as possession by evil spirits and exorcism was tried. The outbreaks lasted for a week at a time, but continued intermittently throughout the fourteenth century. Another serious outbreak happened in 1318 at Strasbourg and the victims were taken for exorcism to the chapel of St Vitus. Everyone involved

— dancers and priests — assumed that evil spirits were responsible, but a modern eye suggests that a deeply rooted insecurity and fear, resulting from memories of the plague of the Black Death may have caused mass hysteria which took this dancing form. St Vitus dance is, today, a popular name for convulsive cholera.

It was from the various examples of possession that happened during this period in history that a list of the classic symptoms of acute demonic attack was made. If all the symptoms appeared in one person at the same time then one would indeed be dealing with an almost unimaginable monster. The states do overlap though, and not all are present at once. Every symptom listed has been observed, either singly or in groups, in many contemporary individuals who have been thought to be possessed.

There are physical changes: the person becomes unrecognizable facially and witnesses see the features of the devil appear; the body becomes wasted and sick, with distended stomach; the complexion alters and the subject suffers from nausea, vomiting, a furred tongue and foul breath. There are internal discomforts, pain and irritation which the victim can only describe as being like an animal eating away at his entrails; sudden pains in the body give the impression of having been inflicted by an external blow; there are convulsions, faints, perhaps a catatonic withdrawal; the voice changes and again witnesses hear the deep gruff voice of the devil. Then there are mental changes: use of language which is described as obscene or filthy and which is always contrary to the expectations or known manner of the victim; there is great aggressiveness revealed in physical violence, insulting and menacing words and behaviour; there is glossolalia, automatic writing (again of a vicious nature), ability to read thoughts of others, knowledge of future events, levitation, instantaneous removal of the person to a far off place, the ability to swivel the head round 360 degrees. And the possessed person radiates a glacial cold. And since we are talking of possession in a Christian context (and, oddly enough, these symptoms seem only to affect Christians) one must add great fear of, and revulsion for, Christ.

With the exception of the three remarkable physical feats mentioned (levitation, astral projection and head-swivelling) every one of these symptoms can be found to have a quite undemonic causation. Exorcists are well aware of this; Fr J. de Tonquedec who acted for the archdiocese of Paris from 1919 to 1939 has written that more than ninety per cent of the cases presented to him were of pseudo-possession. This term means that while the symptoms are probably the same as those for genuine demonic possession the cure lies, not in exorcism but with the psychiatrist whose treatment is accompanied by a religious perspective from supportive priests.

Psychosomatic medicine was a late-comer to the field of inquiry because for many years the philosophy of Descartes which emphasized a complete division between body and soul was so widely adhered to. Thus the idea of physical manifestations of a mental illness was completely unknown (unlike today when almost every illness is labelled psychosomatic even straightforward accidents.)

A substantial proportion of the celebrated cases of possession from the fifteenth to seventeenth centuries were probably due entirely to physical causes. Epilepsy was known to most people, but it can take some deceptive forms. And who knows how many brain tumours, cancerous growths and orthopaedic illnesses caused enduring physical agony attended by frightening physical effects? Then there are the natural but unknown and therefore unregulated abilities of the human mind which are only today being discovered and explored: hypnosis, telepathy, telekinesis, E.S.P. and the entire workings of the sub-conscious.

As far as pseudo-possession is concerned, probably the three major psychological causes could be grouped under the headings of paranoia, hysteria and the externalization of an inner conflict. To the contemporary reader, able to stretch out and grab his paperback Freud to help him through his depressions, it is difficult to pitch himself into the atmosphere of those times, of a world trapped between the two over-riding fears of the Church — its strictures and its wrath — and the devil — his blandishments and his evil. With no knowledge of the workings of the mind and hardly any of the body, in a world riddled with superstition it would take only one unbalanced person to set off a chain reaction, touching the lurking fears and hysteria of others.

Psychiatrists tell us that the reasons for paranoia and hysteria are either the subject's fear, or his desire to attract attention to himself (or more probably, herself). A paranoiac believes that a person, or a group of people, is conspiring against him and will try to produce evidence of this in the form of physical symptoms, if the accusation is against a witch for example. Thus the quite genuine fear of witchcraft and devilry would promote this kind of accusation, backed by the appropriate manifestations.

The hysteric reverses this process; he or she produces the symptoms then seeks a scapegoat. It appears that quite often the hysteric does realize, at some level, that the symptoms are self-induced and therefore finds it necessary to produce a particularly good story to back them up. In this context the devil himself could hardly be a more suitable and unquestionable cause.

It is possible to cast the progress of the sort of cases of possession that occurred in the convents of the sixteenth and seventeenth centuries in the form of a game as outlined by Eric Berne in *Games People Play*. This one could be called *Holier than Thou*. In a group or community of people who are dedicated to perfection, one person feels that she is not appreciated enough for the dedication and devotion she is displaying. Her conscience (Parent) is not strong enough to control the impulses of her resentment (Rebellious Child) nor can she mobilize her reason (Adult) to see the situation as it really is. The game is set in motion by the most appropriate means for the period and context: hysterical symptoms appear. Concern and interest is shown, so the symptoms become more pronounced. The person may have a victim in mind from the beginning, or one may be suggested by the discussion that goes on around her. The climax is reached with excited performances of mass exorcisms and the payoff is achieved with the execution of the victim, whereupon the player can resume her normal demeanour confident that she is now far more blessed than anyone else since she has been selected by the devil for attention, has fought him, won the battle and exposed his agent. The game is played for the benefit of the person's peers, not for outsiders or any accidental interloper.

To work properly, such a Bernian game has to be played by the victim as well as by the persecutor and in *Holier than Thou* the victim would be in an extremely vulnerable position especially in an age when an accusation more or less implied guilt. It is not irrelevant that today, forms of this game are observed among the poor, blacks and members of oppressed sub-cultures. As we have already seen the nuns in particular were not only sexually repressed, but socially oppressed as women.[3]

The externalization of an inner conflict can also manifest itself in phenomena which could be interpreted as possession. Generally the term conflict is felt to mean indecision as to whether to do this, or that. But in reality it is far more acute than that; in fact the implicit idea of choice barely exists for the person. He is the subject of two opposing forces or signals that affect him, as it were, simultaneously. Thus, again using a nun like Jeanne des Anges as an example, the person could well be suffering a tremendous conflict over her sexuality. All her training, discipline and belief cries 'no'; while at the same time her body and her emotions are crying 'yes'. Such conflicts have been known to reveal themselves in unexpected ways, sometimes by malicious or wayward acts, sometimes by self-inflicted wounds (which the person will deny responsibility for) and often by psychosomatic symptoms such as eczema or asthma. The possibility of convulsions and erotic gesture is not so remote.

A. R. G. Owen has suggested[4] that the apparently Satanic persecution of the Cure of Ars was a similar externalization; in his case the conflict was between a longing for solitude and the necessity to continue his arduous pastoral duties. This remarkable man, Jean-Marie-Baptiste Viannay is the patron saint of parish priests. He was born in 1786 and developed considerable psychic gifts. He possessed great talent as a confessor and by the time of his death in 1859 it is estimated that 100,000 pilgrims visited Ars annually. To many people he was a saint on earth — his beatification actually took place in 1904. For fourteen years from 1824 the Curé suffered periodic persecutions that included noises, blows, hammerings, voices, diabolical speech. A holy picture was defaced and his bed was shaken and pulled across the room while he was in it. This is usually taken as an example of poltergeist phenomena with a spiritual significance due to the Curé's work.

The attentions of a frightening but less malicious poltergeist disturbed the home and family of the young John Wesley which, again, may have been symptomatic of internal spiritual tensions. Poltergeist activity is not really understood though many people have tried to produce convincing explanations. The general view today seems to be that the activity — throwing small domestic objects about, displacing pictures, knockings — emanate from a person, usually a child, and are backed by obscure natural causes. However, as John Richards has pointed out, the objects that move round tend not to obey natural laws — that is, things fall slowly, or go round corners.

This survey of the most likely physical and mental causes of possession still leaves open the question of genuine possession, the last ten per cent that Fr de Tonquedec was asked to treat. Is there, in fact, a small percentage of individuals who really are possessed by a personality that is not their own? In his book *But Deliver Us From Evil,* John Richards quotes a passage from R. D. Laing's *The Divided Self* in which the distinguished authority on schizophrenia and radical psychiatrist writes:

A most curious phenomenon of the personality, one which has been observed for centuries, but which has not yet received its full explanation, is that in which the individual seems to be the vehicle of a personality that is not his own. Someone else's personality seems to 'possess' him and be finding expression through his words and actions, whereas the individual's own personality is temporarily 'lost' or 'gone'. This happens with all degrees of malignancy.

In context Mr Richards seems to be using this passage to support his own argument that possession does exist, in fact the whole tone of his book is that the concept does exist, or rather, that Mr Richards *wants* it to exist. But to me the impression Dr Laing gives is that the full explanation *will* be found sooner or later. Discovery has by no means reached a full stop. In concrete imagery one might say that there is a door in the mind; it can be opened by various means — particularly through the use of drugs such as lysergic acid — but it does not open out to external forces, but opens into other parts of the mind. The answer must be sought within man.

YOUR MIND IS ALL YOU HAVE

Exorcism is a form of therapy for the unbalanced mind, and like any form of therapy, be it aspirin or psychiatric analysis, it can be used effectively only in certain, clearly defined circumstances: neither aspirin, nor exorcism is going to do much for a fractured femur. As in psychoanalysis, the attitude of the person possessed is of particular importance to the success of the therapy.

How then does exorcism work? Does Christ really step in and remove or bind an actual demon that has been making his home in a person? Or does the exorcist, as William Sargant persuasively argues, create a special kind of emotional crisis that enables the patient's old behaviour pattern to break down, and a new one to be created?[1]

The conditions required to produce a state of possession are twofold. First, an already existing state of intra-psychic tension in the individual. Second, a particular combination of circumstances that precipitate the tension into a visible explosion. It has also been argued, incidentally, that there can be no possession without consent, however deeply buried in the consciousness that consent might be.

This analysis rejects any possibility of an objective, outside entity being responsible for the state, and places alleged possession firmly in the psychological area of strain and stress. It also suggests that every human being carries within him the potential for being possessed, since everyone is prey to emotion, fear, doubt and degree of despair, which increase suggestibility, and capable of the extremes of utter panic or total withdrawal.

Most people are normally able to control their emotions reasonably effectively because they are sufficiently self-aware. Thus the person who suffers from claustrophobia simply avoids lifts, cellars and pot-holing; and the person who is easily frightened avoids horror movies, seances and roller-coasters. While the person whose emotions are swiftly aroused might enjoy weeping and actively seek opportunities to weep by going to hear music that will affect him accordingly.

Thus a possessive state will emerge when the precipitating factors are unexpected, or when the individual feels that they are there all the time and that he has no control over them, as with the acute paranoiac, who is the helpless victim of a huge conspiracy in which policemen, colleagues and neighbours all play their part.

Attempts have been made to define the type of person most likely to become possessed. Historical examples indicate a heavy preponderance of women and children and the popular belief remains that demon possession is largely limited to women, particularly illiterate and sexually deprived women. In his essay on diabolic possession, Jean Vinchon writes: '. . . we can distinguish two fundamental obsessions of the possessed. There is the obsession or moral solitude to which is joined the obsession of inferiority, frequent with spinsters, with widows, with people who live on the fringe of life, having neither family nor home, with certain religions and nuns, ill-adapted to the cloister which they have entered, not by vocation, but as a result of some previous disappointment. Such morally isolated beings make up a fairly high percentage of the cases of diabolical possession.'[2]

Fr Christopher Neil-Smith, in his book, *The Exorcist and the Possessed*, however, widens the field considerably.

He writes: 'I have also had the privilege to minister exorcism personally to lawyers, both barristers and solicitors . . . architects, surveyors, engineers and designers . . . actually highly intelligent art and book critics as well as TV producers have been exorcized . . .' In reciting this, Fr Neil-Smith is affirming that possession is not the exclusive province of low-class, illiterate females.

Nevertheless it does seem that highly emotionally-charged religious movements tend to attract the least educated and socially deprived individuals. A similar motive may lie behind many people's attraction towards the occult; people who, in Vinchon's phrase, live 'on the fringe of life' and desire to feel that they belong somewhere and to someone. Such people are likely to be emotionally frail and much more susceptible to introspection and neuroses than say, a busy married woman or an active young father.

Unfortunately such people are kept 'on the fringe of life' quite ruthlessly by the social structures and attitudes of the world in which we live. Vinchon talks about 'the obsession of inferiority' as if it is all in the imagination of the spinster or the widow. On the contrary, it is all too real. Career women who compete in a man's world on men's terms and women who seek a political analysis through Womens' Liberation movements, represent only a minute fraction of the female population who are all too aware of their secondary status in society.

The women who does not have the protection of a man, who is unmarried or divorced or a widow, finds herself excluded from the majority of social outlets. Society is constructed — emotionally as well as economically — around the family unit, a concept that the Church promotes. Little wonder, therefore that some lonely women feel excluded and turn to occult groups in a pathetic attempt to contact the spirit of a dead loved one, or to find some sort of human contact denied elsewhere.

Some form of sexual anxiety has been present in virtually all the known cases of possession. One is tempted to say *all* cases, but since so many examples are given only superficially ('She was possessed. I exorcized her. She was cured.'), it is impossible to be dogmatic. Jean Lhermitte has written: '. . . we must observe that if psychoanalysis frequently brings to light some sexual disorder in patients suffering from demonopathy, it is because in their eyes the greatest sin lies in carnal failings of perversions, the most serious of which is homosexuality.'[3]

The attitude of the Christian Church to sex has often been direct: any form of sexual desire or sexual expression that lies outside heterosexual coitus in the context of a monogamous marriage is sinful. And yet the possession-exorcism cycle clearly indicates that no matter how rigorously the Church applies this standard and promotes it, the Judeo-Christian ethic has never been able to control the natural instincts which often manifest themselves irrespective of the prevailing culture. What it has often succeeded in doing is in creating a profound oppression which frequently leads to acute anxiety situations for those who wish to adhere to Christianity but seem, despite themselves, to be sinfully transgressing.

Jean Lhermitte describes such a case. The man in question, brought up in a religious college, had always been haunted by problems of sex and had 'given himself up to solitary sexual practices' (masturbation) 'with some tendency to homosexuality'. He married, 'had some lapses' but never homosexual ones. But he was 'tormented by certain obsessions' (presumably homosexual fantasies) which he tried to counter by 'taking refuge' (evading the real issue) in prayer, penance and spiritual struggle. The symptoms of severe mental disturbance follow with the hearing of voices screaming obscenities at him and visions — 'scenes of utterly unbridled eroticism reminiscent of the temptations of St Anthony, but with no specific and individual feature. All these orgies were characterized by a brazen homosexuality.' The man in question was lucky to be tortured only with voices and visions. The lives of many similarly repressed homosexuals, who feel that marriage and prayer are going to bring about some cure, too often end in tragedy.

The fundamentalist attitude towards sexuality operates in two ways. First, as in the case just recited, a particularly devout individual perceiving signs of what he regards as sexual irregularities in his behaviour, may well come to the conclusion that he is possessed and act out further symptoms. While the priest talking over problems with a troubled person may himself be so shocked by the person's revelation of sexual needs that he concludes that the person is possessed by the devil. F.X. Maquart asks: 'Why is it that the priest, faced with this kind of thing, is so ready to conclude the presence of the devil?'[4] Because, he suggests, by his training and function the priest is used to passing moral judgments. 'The question he asks is: Virtuous or vicious? whereas he ought to ask: Normal or abnormal?' Sound common sense until one realizes the problems facing the priest in ascertaining what is sexually normal or abnormal.

Lhermitte offers another example. A young nun was assailed by 'sexual trials' from the age of fifteen. 'Her director unwisely told her that the devil was at work...' which exacerbated the situation into the wildest excesses of demonic fits. Repeated exorcisms were useless but electric-shock treatment was tried. 'After *one month* of this she was completely free of all ideas of demonic possession.' Lhermitte does not, however, say whether the sexual 'trials' had ceased. Had the director told the young nun that it was not unnatural to masturbate and to have sexual desire for men and that no amount of vows and wimples would alter that, she might have been spared the vindictive assaults of exorcism and electro-therapy.

Similarly, priests have been shocked by the spates of obscenities that gush from the lips of possessed girls and women. This reflects not only a fixed attitude to sex but also male chauvinistic expectations of women and assumptions about their subservient role in society which assume that they cannot possibly *know* such words. Relevant here is the basic fact that the words in our vocabularies that describe the genitals and sexual activity are all socially unacceptable. Fr Neil-Smith in an extra-ordinary self-revealing passage remarks: 'Naturally, un-cleanness is often associated with sex . . .' Perhaps only a Judeo-Christian culture will assume a *natural* link be-tween sex and dirt. Of course, if people are told often enough and firmly enough that sex is nasty, dirty and ugly, then they will surely come to believe it.

A strong sexual element has featured largely in many of the exorcisms performed by Fr Neil-Smith: lesbianism, male homosexuality, masturbation and something he calls mysteriously 'a weird form of oral sex' crop up on many pages of his book.

Fr Neil-Smith's memoir and the Revd John Richards' *But Deliver Us From Evil* are, in their different ways, significant contributions to our knowledge of exorcism. The first is written from the point of view of first-hand experience and makes no attempt to explain anything. It does, however, give us some insight into the way in which cultural misconceptions and social distortion can affect the exorcist as well as the possessed.

The second book is written from a highly practical, pastoral standpoint and its technical information is extremely useful and interesting. Both men are, however, dimly aware of the dangerous dichotomy between a fundamentalist Christian attitude to sex and the facts of sex itself. Neither explores the possibility of a social or political analysis of the situation but instead reinforces oppressive standards. Fr Neil-Smith writes: 'The danger of the permissive society is that it tends to give the impression that it no longer matters what form of sex is used'. There he is surely wrong. One of the impulses behind what he misleadingly calls the 'permissive society' is that to many people it matters very much what form of sex is used and people were getting extremely frustrated because they were continually being told what forms of sex they couldn't use.

Mr Richards says more or less the same thing only with slightly more grace: '. . . our present uncritical acceptance of thinly disguised doctrines that the abnormal, the immoral, and the wrong are *really* the normal, the moral and the right, certainly cause Screwtape (the devil) to chuckle with delight. . .' The basic underestimation of the morality of sexual liberation is coupled with the charge that any argument that tends to contest a tenet of Christianity is automatically of the devil and should not therefore be listened to.

But from St Jerome trying to burn his sexual desires black in the desert sun, to the teenage girl possessed by sexual desire for a dead pop star, the annals of possession resound with the message that the sexual instincts will not be governed by man-made rules and regulations. And if these rules cannot be broken without guilt, then the most appalling mental and physical damage results.

I have laid particular emphasis in this chapter on the

sexual element in possession because such a significant number of recorded cases suggest it to be a dominating characteristic, and indeed it is recognized as such by many exorcists. It is not, however, an invariable denominator. Some individuals who have been afflicted with possession seem to have been motivated by what is called the diva complex — a desire for fame and admiration disproportionate to their intrinsic worth. This is particularly marked in the case of Sister Jeanne des Anges later in life as she cultivated her celebrity.

One of the facets of demonic attack is that deliverance is possible in the name of Christ. Clearly, this cannot be ascertained until after exorcism, but it does provide a pointer towards the sort of situation in which exorcism may be said to work. Both the exorcist and the possessed must share the conviction that the problem is of a spiritual nature and that it can only be relieved by spiritual means.

In *The Mind Possessed*, Dr William Sargant has described in detail experiments he conducted just after the Second World War in the treatment of men suffering from battle neurosis. By the use of drugs, Dr Sargant was able to make men emotionally relive the experiences which caused their breakdown. The effect was to induce in the patients intense nervous excitement and violent outbursts of emotion after which there would be an emotional collapse. Later the patients would recover feeling more like their normal selves and with the ability to look back on their memories without any attendant fear and anxiety.

Dr Sargant linked this experience with various forms of spirit possession which he has witnessed in different parts of the world, as well as with the effects of drugs, alcohol and sex. He was able to chart a scale of possession ranging from the earliest symptoms through to a climax followed by a relapse and a return to normality as happens when the Voodoo god, the *loa*, mounts a worshipper.

Many people argue that exorcism has exactly this effect on the possessed person. That it is able to work in a highly suggestive way and create an emotional climax followed by a return to normal, the old fear and oppressions vanquished. If this is the case, then exorcism does not have to be Christian to be effective. Provided all involved share the same belief, it can be pagan occult or even improvised.

Nevertheless, some kind of aftercare is always necessary, especially if the patient has been suffering for some time before the exorcism. This is quite properly catered to in the Christian context where the priest is urged to lead the patient back to a devout life of witness and through this he receives essential social and spiritual support.

The mind-body-spirit triumvirate still remains to a large extent, split up; each component has its own ministry and meetings between them have been rare. In recent years, however, there has been an increasing tendency for psychiatrists and doctors to refer patients to exorcists.

The question of evil remains — and will always remain. Only a minority today believe in individual demons but elements within a society which threaten to disrupt the *status quo* or effect an imbalance will be dubbed as evil. Communism, drug taking, violation of the traditional Christian ethic, pop music, property development, exploitation, strikes, pollution, war and nuclear fission. . . all are firmly labelled as evil by one section of society or another. Some of these may indeed be highly undesirable, others less so. The fact remains that what man fears he tends to demonize, to see as the work of the devil.

However, it is also an inescapable fact that there are some cases of possession which are not susceptible to purely psychological or emotional reasoning and treatment. And it may well be that these are cases of possession needing the skilled attention of the exorcist.

NOTES

INTRODUCTION

1 'Exorcism' in *Man, Myth and Magic* (Purnell 1971) p. 872.
2 Petitpierre, Dom Robert, ed., *Exorcism Report* (S.P.C.K. 1972) p. 9.
3 *The Times.* 5 July 1974.
4 *Exorcism Report,* p. 10.

CHAPTER 1

1 Johann Weyer, quoted by Eric Maple in 'Evil Spirits in Europe' in *Man, Myth and Magic,* p. 862.
2 Quoted by E. O. James in *The Nature and Function of Priesthood* (Thames & Hudson 1955) p. 52.

CHAPTER 2

1 *Exorcism Report,* p. 15.
2 Quoted by G. B. Gardner in *The Meaning of Witchcraft* (Aquarian 1959) p. 111.
3 *Exorcism Report,* p. 13.
4 D. F. Strauss, *The Life of Jesus Critically Examined* (S.C.M. 1973) p. 423 ff.

CHAPTER 3

1 St Cyprian, St Augustine and Minucius Felix, quoted by Eric Maple in *The Domain of Devils.* Robert Hale 1966.
2 Maple, ibid.
3 Derrick Sherwin Bailey, *The Man-Woman Relation in Christian Thought.* Longman 1959.
4 Maple, ibid.
5 Gillian Tyndall, 'Hysterical Possession and Witchcraft' in *Man, Myth and Magic,* p. 1382.

CHAPTER 4

1 Paul Tillich, 'The Lost Dimension in Religion' in *Adventures of the Mind.* Gollancz 1958.

2 Quoted in *Tatler* Special on Exorcism, Spring 1974.

CHAPTER 5

1 Quoted by Francoise Strachan in *Casting out the Devils.* Aquarian 1972.
2 F. J. Sheed, *Soundings in Satanism*. Mowbray 1972.

CHAPTER 6

1 Strachan, ibid.

CHAPTER 7

1 *Sunday People.* 17 March 1974.
2 'Satanism Today' in *Soundings in Satanism.*
3 John Richards, *But Deliver us from Evil.* Darton, Longman & Todd 1974.
4 Sheed, ibid.
5 *Tatler* Special.

CHAPTER 8

1 Francis Huxley, 'Drugs' in *Man, Myth and Magic*, p. 711.
2 William Sargant, *The Mind Possessed.* Heinemann 1973.
3 See also, Eric Berne, *Games People Play.* Deutsch 1966.
4 *Man, Myth and Magic*, p. 577.

CHAPTER 9

1 Sargant, ibid.
2 Sheed, ibid.
3 ibid.
4 ibid.
5 ibid.

A GLOSSARY OF EXORCISM

Amulet	A charm to ward off evil spirits, worn round the neck or possibly attached to the windows or doors of a house
Animism	The projection of souls or personalities onto animals and inanimate objects
Arcane	Mysterious; hidden
Asmodeus	Demon who provokes erotic fantasies
Bacchae	Followers of Dionysus; usually intoxicated and sexually excited
Black Mass	A ritual which reverses the processes of the Roman Catholic Mass; used to worship the devil
Charm	An incantation spoken to drive away evil spirits
Deevs	Persian spirits
Demon	A malevolent spiritual being
Demonology	The scientific study of demons
Demoniac	A person who is possessed by a demon (see Possession)
Devil	Another word for Demon
Devil, the	The supreme spirit of evil (see Satan)
Dionysus	Greek god of wine
Ecstacy	A state of trance associated with communication with the gods
Enthusiasm	Conviction of the inward presence of the divine
Erzulie	The Voodoo goddess of beauty
E.S.P.	Extra-sensory perception involving phenonema such as thought-reading

Exorcist	A person who uses a specific ritual to expel evil spirits
Glossolalia	Speaking in tongues; the sudden ability to speak in an unknown language
Holy Water	A mixture of water and salt, each of which is first exorcized and blessed separately, to be used by a priest
Horned God	Worshipped by witches, a god associated with the countryside (see Pan)
Isaacaron	Demon who provokes masturbation
Lilith	Desert demon, sometimes assuming the guise of a screech-owl, particularly malevolent to Jewish babies
Loa	The name given to a Voodoo god or goddess
Magician	A person who uses magic
Malleus Maleficarum	A book, *The Hammer of Witches* written by Heinrich Kramer and Jacob Sprengler in 1484, being a guide to witch hunting
Mesmerism	A form of rudimentary hypnosis developed by Franz Mesmer c 1766
Occult	Hidden knowledge
Pan	Roman god associated with the countryside; plays pipes, has horns, hoofs, and a tail (see Horned God)
Pazuzu	Particularly vindictive and dangerous Babylonian demon associated with malaria
Pentecostal	Revivalist form of worship based on the belief that baptism by the Holy Spirit makes itself manifest, usually by outbreaks of speaking in tongues or enthusiasm

Poltergeist	A noisy ghost who throws things around a house
Possession	A state in which a person seems to be taken over by another entity
Rituale Romanum	The Roman Catholic rubrics, or instructions, for exorcists
Satan	The supreme spirit of evil: referred to as The Devil
Satanist	One who worships Satan and has usually made a pact with him
Shaman	A sorcerer-priest of primitive societies who consciously induces spirits to possess him
Shimrah	An amulet specifically to protect Jewish children from Lilith
Tantric	An ancient Indian cult which uses sexual intercourse as a means of communicating with the spirits
Telekinesis	The ability of a person to move objects without touching them; always unconscious and uncontrolled
Trident of Paracelsus	A triple-pronged sword used by magicians to exorcize spirits by stabbing them
Vampire	A spirit that feeds on the blood of living human beings
Voodoo	Religious cult of Haiti of which possession by the spirit is the focus (see Loa)
Witch	A person who cultivates supernatural powers and is an agent of the devil. Or, a person who adheres to an antique fertility cult
Zar	An Ethiopian spirit that tends to possess humans

BIBLIOGRAPHY

(A selection of books which have been useful, though not an exhaustive list.)

Bataille, Georges, *Eroticism*. John Calder 1962.

Blatty, William Peter, *The Exorcist*. Corgi 1974.

Gardner, G.B., *The Meaning of Witchcraft*. Aquarian 1959.

Hole, Christina, *Witchcraft in England*. Collier 1968.

The Holy Bible

James, E.O., *The Nature and Function of Priesthood*. Thames & Hudson 1955.

King, Francis, *Ritual Magic*. New English Library 1972.

Kolakowski, Leszek, *The Devil and Scripture*. Oxford University Press 1973.

Maple, Eric, *The Domain of Devils*. Robert Hale 1966.

Neil-Smith, Christopher, *The Exorcist and the Possessed*. James Pike 1974.

Parrinder, Geoffrey, *Witchcraft*. Penguin 1958.

Petitpierre, Dom Robert, ed., *Exorcism Report*. S.P.C.K. 1972.

The Radical Therapist, essays edited by the Radical Therapist Collective. Penguin 1974.

Richards, John, *But Deliver Us From Evil*. Darton, Longman & Todd 1974.

Sargant, William, *The Mind Possessed*. Heinemann 1973.

Seabrook, William, *Witchcraft*. Harrap 1940.

Sheed, F.J., ed., *Soundings in Satanism*. Mowbray 1972.

Sladek, John, *The New Apocrypha*. Hart-Davis Mac-Gibbon 1973.

Strachan, Francoise, *Casting out the Devils*. Aquarian 1972.

St Clair, David, *Drum and Candle.* Belmont/Tower 1971.

Strauss, David Friedrich, *The Life of Jesus Critically Examined.* S.C.M. 1973.

Taylor, G. Rattray, *Sex in History.* Panther 1965.

Thomson, Robert, *The Pelican History of Psychology.* Pelican 1968.

Watts, Alan W., *Myth and Ritual in Christianity.* Thames & Hudson 1953.

Woodward, Christopher, *Healing Through Faith.* Priory Press 1973.

Yarnold, E., *The Awe-Inspiring Rites of Initiation.* St Paul 1971.

INDEX